SKILLFUL

LITTLE

FINGERS

BOOK I

Developing Grace and Technique

Through 40+ Exercises

In Chopin's Position

For Piano Beginners

Ages 5 – 12

By REENA YOUNG

SKILLFUL LITTLE FINGERS:
Developing Grace and Technique through 40+ Exercises in Chopin's Position

Copyright © **2000–2026** Irina Younger Published under the pen name **Reena Young**

Published by IVY Music Publishing

Exercises composed in 2000, first published in 2025.

ISBN: 979-8-9944452-0-4

For permissions or inquiries, please contact: **Email:** reenayoung99@gmail.com

Printed in the United States of America

Book cover designed by Reena Young using elements and templates from Canva.com

Table of Contents

Prelude

How Chopin Found Me

From my earliest memories, music felt as if it were woven into me. Before I could read, before I understood what "talent" meant, I sang grown-up songs with clear pitch and natural phrasing, as if melody were simply another language I already knew. My parents noticed this immediately. They often exchanged glances—half surprised, half amused—whenever I sang along to the radio with uncanny accuracy for a child my age.

To them, it was obvious: I would start attending a music school.

That is how my piano life began—not with discipline or ambition, but with a quiet confidence my family had in me long before I understood anything about technique or practice. I was a small girl, eager to place my hands on the keys, to feel how sound vibrated under my fingertips, to explore this instrument that felt both mysterious and familiar. Only later did the reality of my environment come into view.

I grew up in the Soviet Union in the 1960s, where children's talents were taken seriously, and music schools demanded rigorous discipline. Mornings belonged to regular school; afternoons to the "musicalka" — piano lessons twice a week, solfège, choir, and music literature. It was a world of strict schedules and big expectations, one that left little room for rest or wandering thoughts. Soviet music schools were famously demanding: some children flourished under that system, others struggled.
I was somewhere in between.

As the years passed, something in me began to shift. The novelty faded. Practice became routine. Technical drills felt mechanical, and the pieces assigned to me rarely stirred my imagination. My hands felt stiff, my sound lifeless. My teacher—kind, patient, and gentle—began offering quiet warnings: if I didn't improve, I might not be allowed to continue.

I wasn't rebellious. I wasn't lazy. I hadn't yet heard the music capable of awakening me.

I worked, I practiced (enough in my opinion), I did everything that was required—yet something essential was missing. The music I played felt dry; scales fell under my fingers like empty patterns. I felt disconnected, as if I were going through the motions without understanding why.

Then everything changed in a single evening.

A visiting pianist from Lithuania, Aleksandra Juozapėnaitė, came to give a recital of Chopin. Concerts like this were rare and felt almost festive. Posters appeared on the streets. Teachers urged their students to attend. I went without much expectation, carrying my music folder because I was supposed to practice afterward.

I remember the moment she walked onto the stage.
She wore an elegant, floor-length concert gown, nothing like I had ever seen in my small town. Her appearance alone seemed to come from another world.

And then she began to play.

The opening piece — something lyrical and luminous — was unlike anything I had heard. The sound felt warm, breathing, alive. It rose and fell like speech, full of shades and colors I didn't know existed. For the first time, I heard a piano not as an instrument of assignments, but as a voice.

But what changed me completely was the Revolutionary Étude (Number 12) near the end of the program. The left hand surged with power, the right hand burned with passion, and the whole hall seemed to vibrate. I sat frozen, breathless, as if the music had carried me somewhere far beyond the world I knew.

When I left the hall, I was silent, shaken, full of something new. Only halfway home did I remember that I had left my music folder on the seat. It didn't matter. I wanted to get home to my piano—urgently, desperately, joyfully.

That night, I practiced not because I had to, but because something inside me had awakened. At my next lesson, my teacher looked at me with gentle astonishment and said,
"You've developed a touch not every student achieves."

From that moment on, there was no doubt: **music would be my calling.**

I began searching for Chopin's music everywhere. There was no internet at the time, so I ordered his scores by mail. When the fancy Paderewski edition finally arrived, it felt like opening a treasure: thick pages, elegant engraving, and photographs of Chopin's manuscripts. Those scores shaped my youth as I finished music school, entered music college, performed, and eventually became a teacher myself.

Years later, life brought me across the ocean to the United States, where I opened my own private piano studio. I taught, learned, and continued to seek clarity and ease in my students' hands.

Then one day, long after that childhood recital, I read about Chopin as a pedagogue. His belief in the natural hand, the curved fingers, the freedom of the wrist, the balance between black and white keys—everything I had once felt without knowing—suddenly had a name: *Chopin's position.*

In that moment, I understood: Chopin had guided me my entire life. First, as a child, discovering beauty. Then, as a young musician, finding inspiration.
And finally, as a teacher, seeking freedom and expression in my students.

This book grows from that lifelong connection.
It is a tribute to the moment music first touched my heart and a guide for teachers and students who seek natural, expressive piano playing.

I hope that among the children who open these pages, another spark will ignite — just as it once did for me.

A Note to the Teacher:

The art of teaching piano has always been closely tied to posture, touch, and the natural relationship between the hand and the keyboard. Among the great pedagogues, Frédéric Chopin occupies a special place. His students recalled that he began technical study not with the "easy" C-major scale, but with keys rich in black notes—B major and Db major—because these positions placed the hand most naturally over the keyboard.

In this so-called *"Chopin's position,"* the longer fingers rest comfortably on the black keys while the thumb and little finger settle on the white keys. This setup creates a natural arch, encourages supple movement, and allows the pianist to play with freedom rather than strain. Both hands benefit from this principle: the right hand finds balance on the grouping **E–F#–G#–A#–B**, while the left hand is equally well supported by beginning on **C–Bb–Ab–Gb–F**.

The present collection of exercises grows directly from that insight. In 2000, I composed these studies for my students to provide young beginners with an immediate experience of the natural hand. Over the years, the exercises have become a central part of my teaching, and the results have been consistently remarkable. My students developed curved fingers, flexible wrists, free-moving elbows, and relaxed shoulders—all essential foundations for healthy, expressive piano playing. By starting from comfort and balance, they avoided the tension that often hampers beginners and instead discovered the joy of a beautiful, singing tone.

This book also introduces young learners to the language of articulation. The exercises incorporate *legato, staccato, and "breath" markings*, weaving musical expression into the earliest stages of technical training. Because the studies rely on finger numbers rather than note reading, children can focus entirely on movement, sound, and touch before the complexity of staff notation is introduced. The approach is particularly suited to the youngest beginners, offering them a playful yet disciplined way into the world of piano. Coloring images on pages may be used as a reward for mastering each exercise.

I offer this book to teachers as both a practical tool and a pedagogical philosophy. Rooted in Chopin's wisdom yet shaped by years of teaching experience, these exercises invite each student into a natural, effortless relationship with the keyboard. My hope is that, as your pupils explore them, they will not only gain a secure technique but also cultivate the relaxed and expressive artistry that Chopin himself so deeply valued.

You'll find more teaching materials at the end of the book.

Wishing you much success,
Reena Young

Dear Student,

Welcome to the piano! This book is your very first step into the beautiful world of music. You are about to learn a special way of holding your hands on the keys called **"Chopin's position."** It was named after Frédéric Chopin, one of the greatest pianists and composers of all time. He discovered that when the longer fingers rest on the black keys, and the shorter ones stay on the white keys, the hands feel comfortable and natural—just like they belong there.

In this position, your fingers will be curved, your wrists flexible, your elbows free, and your shoulders relaxed. That means your hands can move easily and beautifully across the keyboard, without stiffness or strain. It's like finding the most comfortable seat in a big chair; it just feels right!

The exercises in this book are simple and fun. You don't need to read music yet; you'll use finger numbers instead. Along the way, you'll also discover little "musical signs" such as *legato* (smooth and connected), *staccato* (short and bouncy), and even *"breath marks"* that show you when to lift your hand like a singer takes a breath.

And here's something special: this book can also be a coloring book! After you master an exercise, you get to color the picture as a reward. That way, your progress will be as colorful as your playing.

I hope these exercises help you feel at home on the piano. With each page, you'll grow stronger, freer, and more expressive. One day, you may even play the beautiful music of Chopin himself!

Happy playing!

Frédérick Chopin

1810 - 1849

Frédérick Chopin was a remarkably talented pianist and composer who played the piano beautifully, wrote wonderful music, and even taught others how to play. He lived about 200 years ago, but people all around the world still love his music today. You might have already heard some of his famous songs! If not, you can use this QR code to watch a video on YouTube with a phone and listen to Chopin's music.

This is a beautiful Waltz in A Minor, played by talented Bruce Liu from Canada. Please scan this QR code with your phone:

Or use this link: Bruce Liu - Waltz in A Minor, B.150 (Chopin)

Let's trace your hands on these two pages!

Place your **left hand** on this page and trace it.

One day, you'll laugh at how tiny your hands were when you first started playing piano.

Note:

All the left-hand (L.H.) exercises will appear on the left-hand page.

Place your **right hand** on this page and trace it.

In the future, you'll have fun comparing your big hands to the tiny ones you traced when you started playing piano.

Note:

All the right-hand (R.H.) exercises will appear on the right-hand page.

Chopin's Position for Left Hand (L.H.)

○ This special way of putting your hand on the keyboard is called *Chopin's Position.*

○ Your short fingers (thumb - 1 and pinky - 5) rest on the white keys, C and F.

○ Your longer fingers (2, 3, and 4) sit nicely on the three black keys.

○ Keep all your fingers curved, even your thumb! The thumb lands on the white key with its side tip.

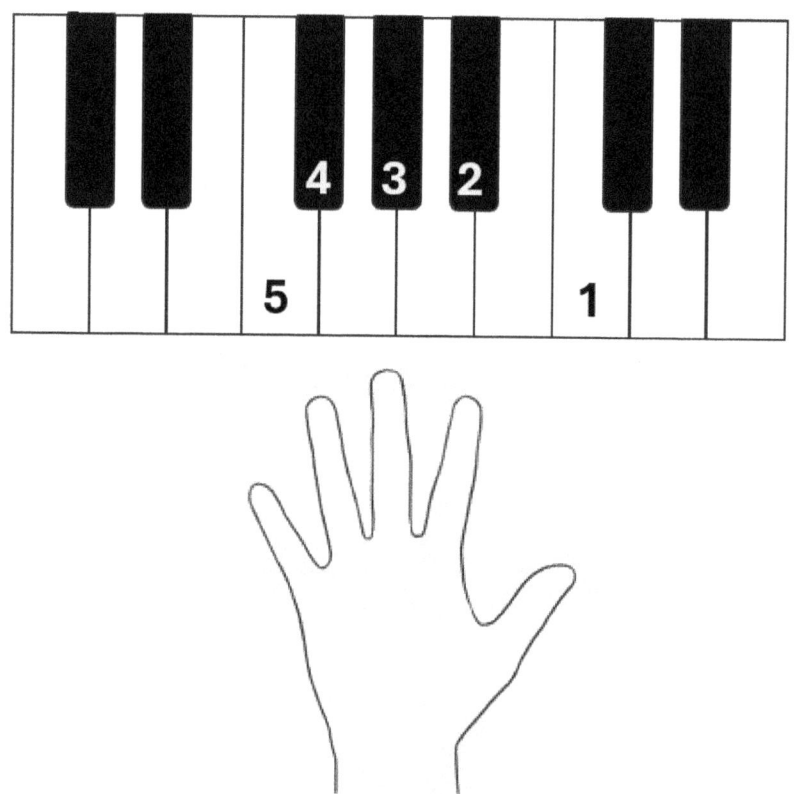

○ Our fingers are tall and short, but when we make a little curve, they stand in a row like best friends. Magic!

Chopin's Position for Right Hand (R.H.)

o This special way of putting your hand on the keyboard is called *Chopin's Position.*

o Your short fingers (thumb - 1 and pinky - 5) rest on the white keys, E and B.

o Your longer fingers (2, 3, and 4) sit nicely on the three black keys.

o Keep all your fingers curved, even your thumb! The thumb lands on the white key with its side tip.

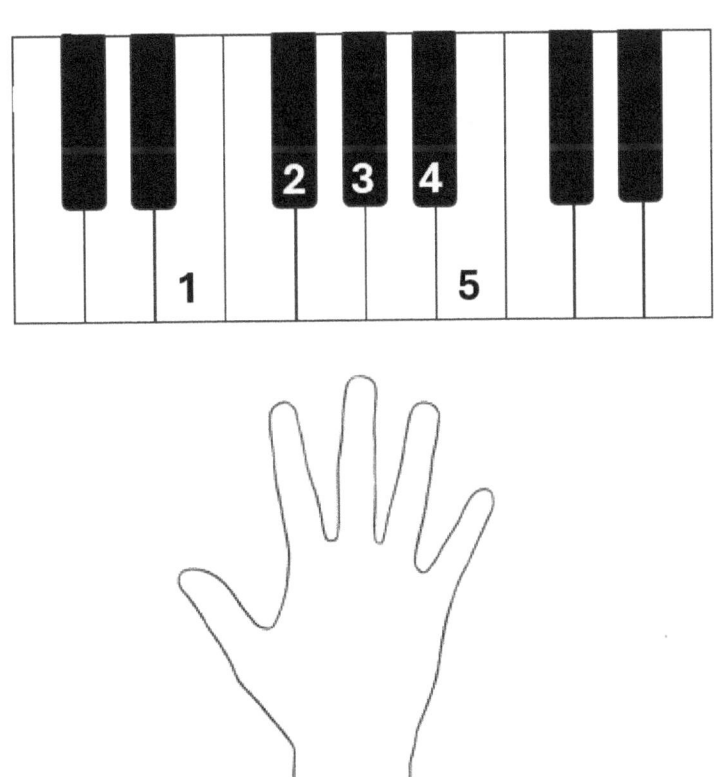

o Even though our fingers are not the same size, curving them makes them equal—like a secret trick your hand can do!

Exercise 1. Climbing the Stairs Down and Up
Left Hand (L.H.)

1. Look at *the time signature* — it's the music's secret code!
2. How many *beats* are in each *measure*?
3. Do you see *bar lines*? *A Double bar line*? How many measures?
4. Clap the rhythm and count it out loud like a drummer.
5. Tap this rhythm on the piano lid. Use correct finger numbers.
6. Next, find your hand's "home" on the keys.
7. Play with ease and count steadily, giving every note time to live its full life. Keep your fingers curved like a cat's paw.
8. Check your wrist: nice and flat, with your elbow floating out a little.
9. After practice, you can color this picture if you wish!

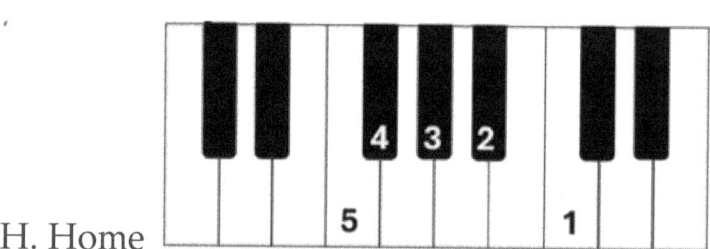

L.H. Home

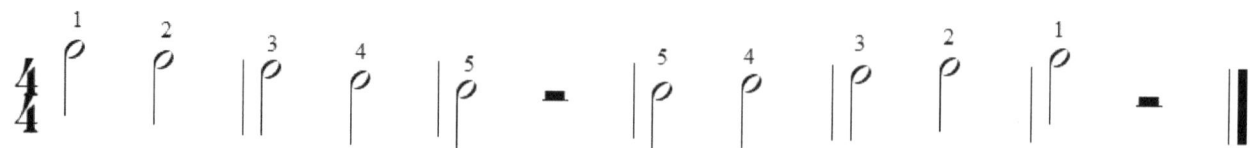

Exercise 2. Climbing the Stairs Up and Down
Right Hand (R.H.)

1. How many beats are in each *measure*?

2. Do you see *bar lines*? *A Double bar line*? How many measures?

3. Clap the rhythm and count it out loud like a drummer.

4. Tap this rhythm on the piano lid and count. Use correct finger numbers.

5. Next, find your hand's "home" on the keys.

6. Play with ease and count steadily, giving every note time to live its full life. Keep your fingers curved like a cat's paw.

7. Check your wrist: nice and flat, with your elbow floating out a little.

8. After practice, you can color this picture if you wish!

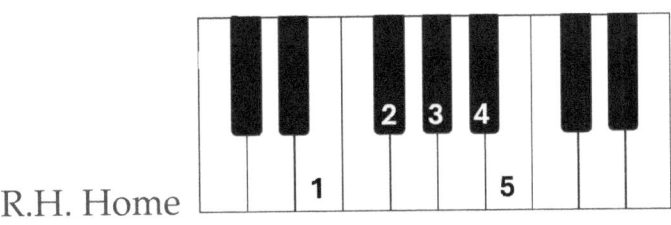

R.H. Home

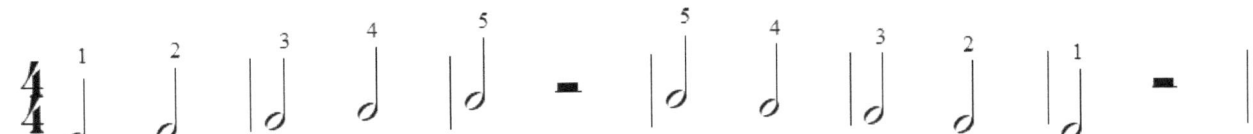

Exercise 3. The Wishing Star Parade   L.H.

Practicing the arm stroke

1. Check the time signature. How many beats are in each measure?
2. Do you see *quarter rests*? How many?
3. Clap the rhythm and count it out loud like a drummer.
4. Play and count this rhythm on the piano lid using a gentle drop of your arm. Use correct finger numbers.
5. Next, find your hand's "home" on the keys.
6. Play each note like you are dropping something soft into the keys. Let your hand fall gently. Keep your fingers curved like a cat's paw.
7. Check your wrist: nice and flat, with your elbow floating out a little.
8. You can color this picture if you wish!

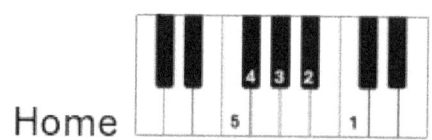

Home

Exercise 4. The Wishing Star Parade R.H.

Practicing the arm stroke

1. Check the time signature. How many beats are in each measure?
2. Do you see *quarter rests*? How many?
3. Clap the rhythm and count it out loud like a drummer.
4. Play and count this rhythm on the piano lid using a gentle drop of your arm. Use correct finger numbers.
5. Next, find your hand's "home" on the keys.
6. Play each note like you are dropping something soft into the keys. Let your hand fall gently. Keep your fingers curved like a cat's paw.
7. Check your wrist: nice and flat, with your elbow floating out a little.
8. You can color this picture if you wish!

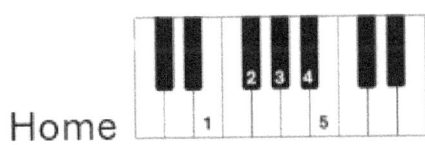

Exercise 5. Knock-knock-knock! L.H.

Practicing the wrist stroke

1. Check the time signature. How many beats are in each measure?
2. Clap the rhythm and count it out loud.
3. Do you see the tiny commas above the notes? Those are called **breath marks**. When you see one, let your hand float up with a little roll of your wrist—forward and upward—like your hand wants to touch the piano lid.
4. There is *a repeat sign* at the end.
5. Play this rhythm on the piano lid. Make a soft knocking motion, using your wrist. Remember the correct finger numbers.
6. Next, find your hand's "home" on the keys.
7. Play and count, making every note live its full life.
8. Keep your fingers curved, like little arches.
9. You can color this picture if you wish!

Home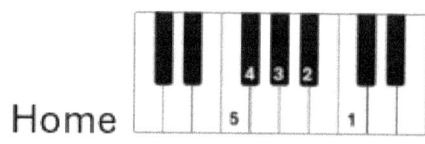

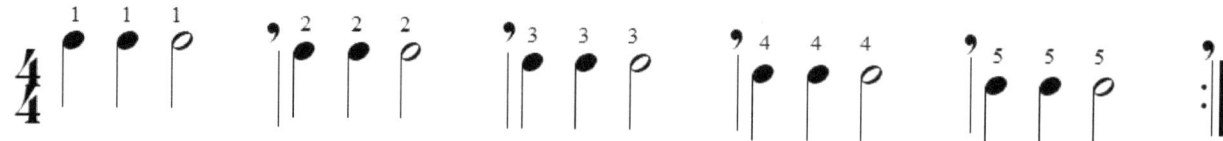

Exercise 6. Knock-knock-knock!   R.H.

Practicing the wrist stroke

1. Check the time signature. How many beats are in each measure?
2. Clap the rhythm and count it out loud.
3. Do you see the tiny commas above the notes? Those are called **breath marks.** When you see one, let your hand float up with a little roll of your wrist—forward and upward—like your hand wants to touch the piano lid.
4. Play this rhythm on the piano lid. Make a soft knocking motion, using your wrist. Remember the correct finger numbers.
5. Next, find your hand's "home" on the keys.
6. Play and count, making every note live its full life.
7. You can color this picture if you wish!

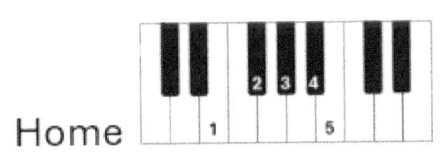

Exercise 7. Building Bridges L.H.

Practicing two notes per stroke

1. Check the time signature. How many beats are in each measure?
2. Clap the rhythm and count it out loud.
3. Do you see the tiny arches above the notes? Those are called *slurs*. They tell you to connect one note to another, playing *legato*.
4. Play this rhythm on the piano lid. Use the correct finger numbers. Tap the first note of the two with a gentle drop of the arm. Then start rolling your wrist forward and play the second note.
5. Play and count, using drop-roll motion in each measure. Listen to the sound your fingers make. The second note sounds a little softer, right?
6. Keep your fingers curved.

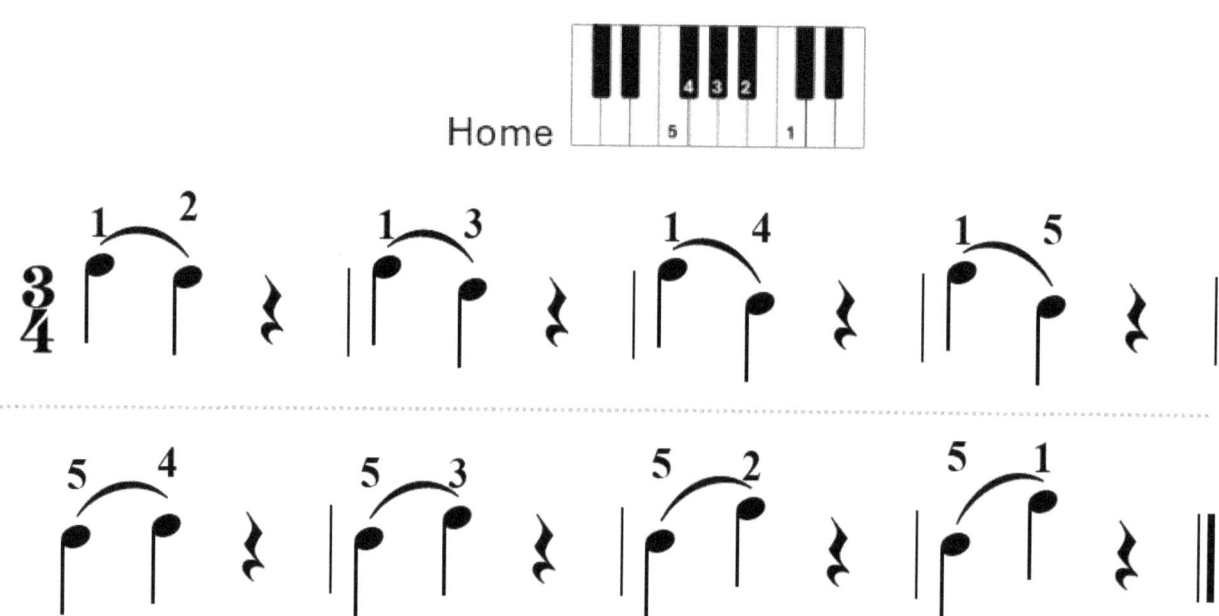

Exercise 8. Building Bridges R.H.

Practicing two notes per stroke

1. Check the time signature. How many beats are in each measure?
2. Clap the rhythm and count it out loud.
3. Do you see the tiny arches below the notes? Those are called **slurs**. They tell you to connect one note to another, playing **legato**.
4. Play this rhythm on the piano lid. Use the correct finger numbers. Tap the first note of the two with a gentle drop of the arm. Then start rolling your wrist forward and play the second note.
5. Play and count, using drop-roll motion in each measure. Listen to the sound your fingers make. The second note sounds a little softer, right?
6. Keep your fingers curved.

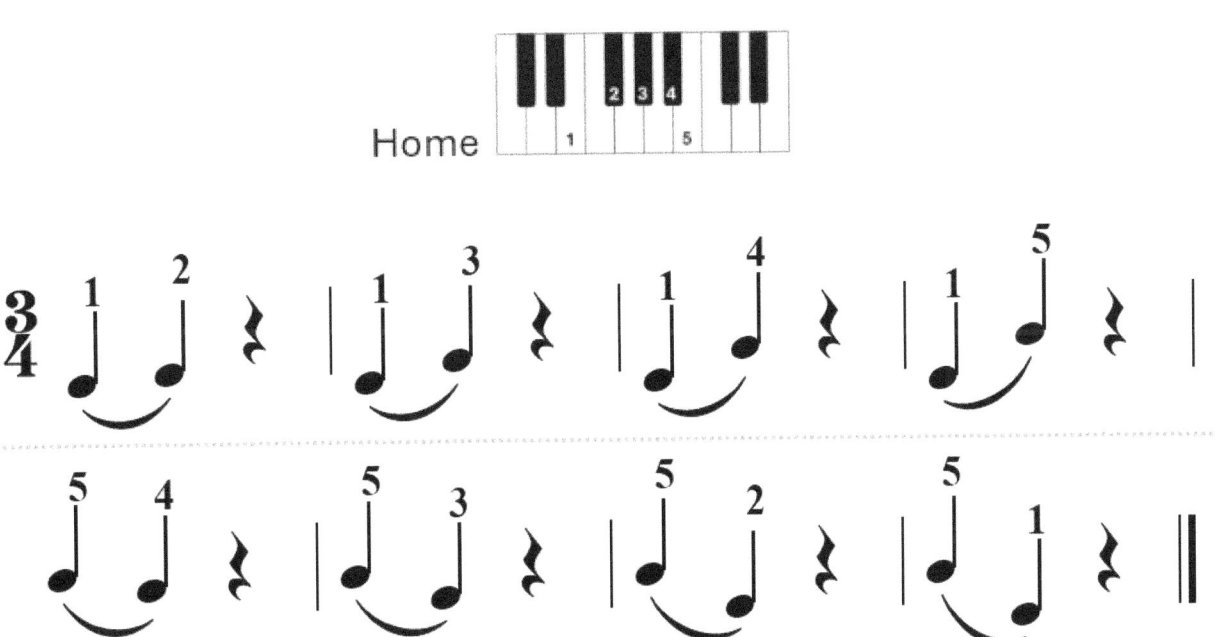

Exercise 9. The Church Bells L.H.

Playing two notes together

1. Check the time signature.
2. Clap the rhythm and count it out loud.
3. Do you see the stacked whole notes? They are played together.
4. Tap this rhythm on the piano lid. Use the correct finger numbers. Tap the first of the two notes with a gentle drop of the arm, then roll your wrist forward to play the second note. After that, play the two whole notes together with good finger support.
5. Play and count. Listen to the sound your fingers make — *ding… dong…* Does it resemble church bells?
6. Keep your fingers curved.

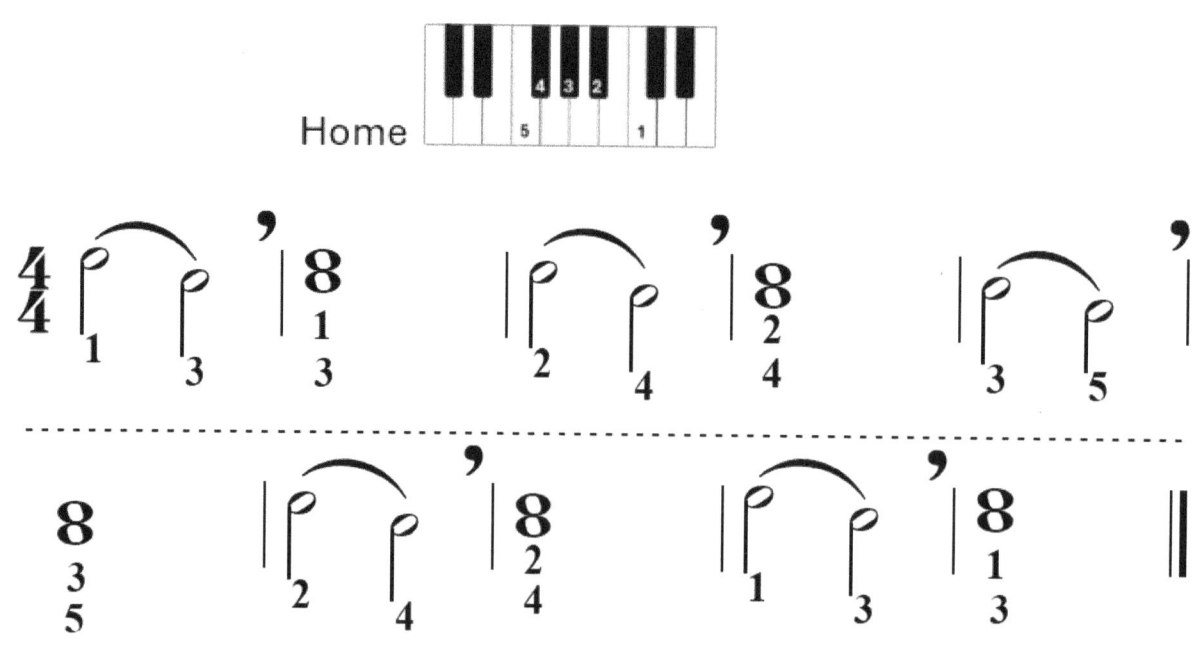

Exercise 10. The Church Bells R.H.

Playing two notes together

1. Check the time signature.
2. Clap the rhythm and count it out loud.
3. Do you see the stacked whole notes? They are played together.
4. Tap this rhythm on the piano lid. Use the correct finger numbers. Tap the first of the two notes with a gentle drop of the arm, then roll your wrist forward to play the second note. After that, play the two whole notes together with good finger support.
5. Play and count. Listen to the sound your fingers make — *ding… dong…* Does it resemble church bells?
6. Keep your fingers curved.

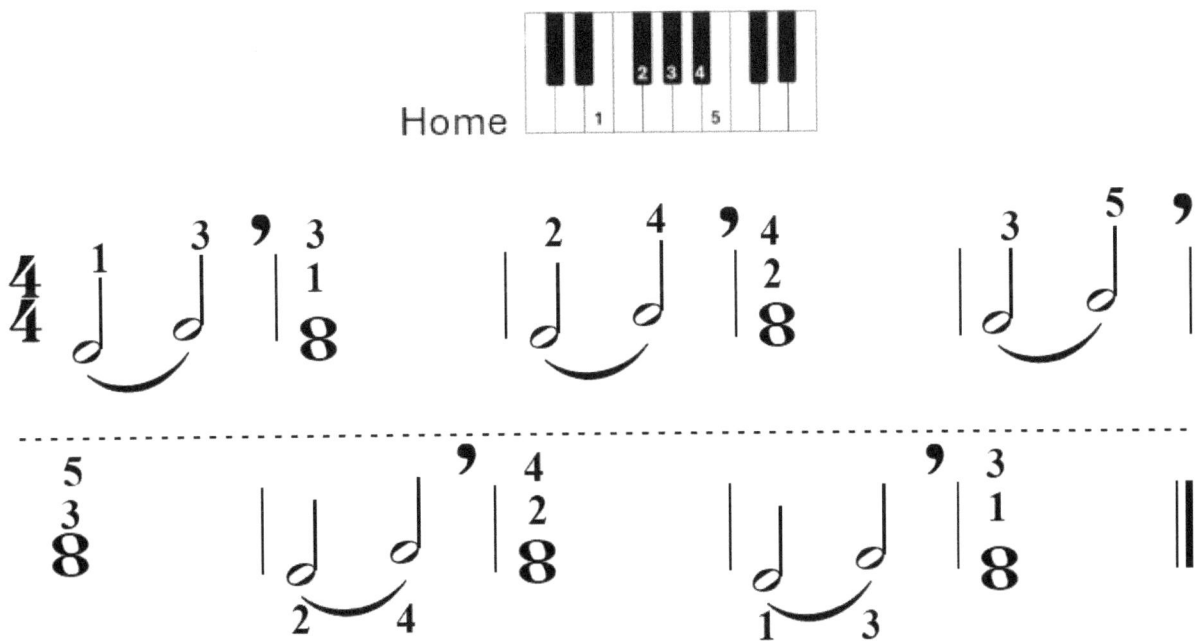

Exercise 11. Playing Ball L.H.

Practicing forearm staccato

1. Check the time signature.
2. Do you see the tiny dots above the notes? Those are *staccato* marks.
3. *Staccato* is played very short — as if you touched something very hot. Your forearm should stay engaged, almost like when you bounce a basketball.
4. Tap the rhythm on the piano lid and count out loud.
5. Play the exercise and count.

Home

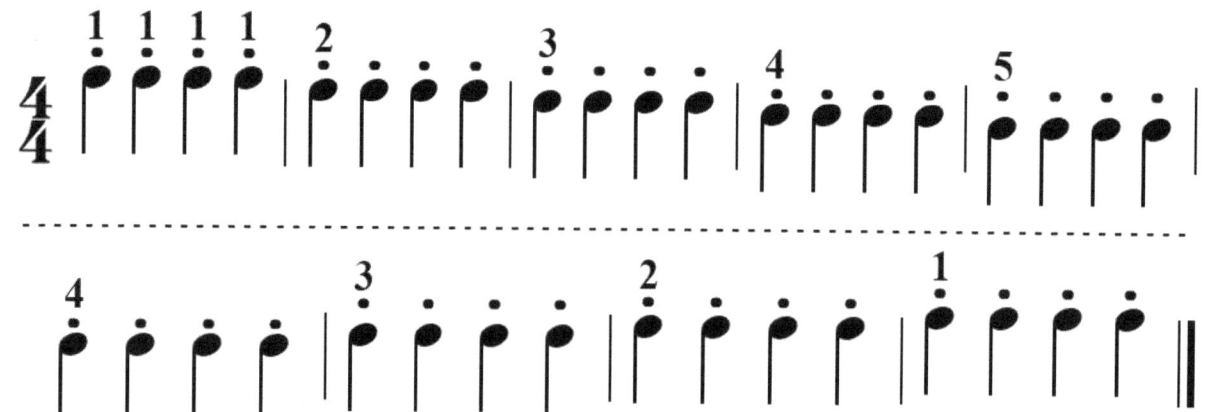

Exercise 12. Playing Ball R.H.

Practicing forearm staccato

1. Check the time signature.
2. Do you see the tiny dots below the notes? Those are *staccato* marks.
3. *Staccato* is played very short — as if you touched something very hot. Your forearm should stay engaged, almost like when you bounce a basketball.
4. Tap the rhythm on the piano lid and count out loud.
5. Play the exercise and count.

Home

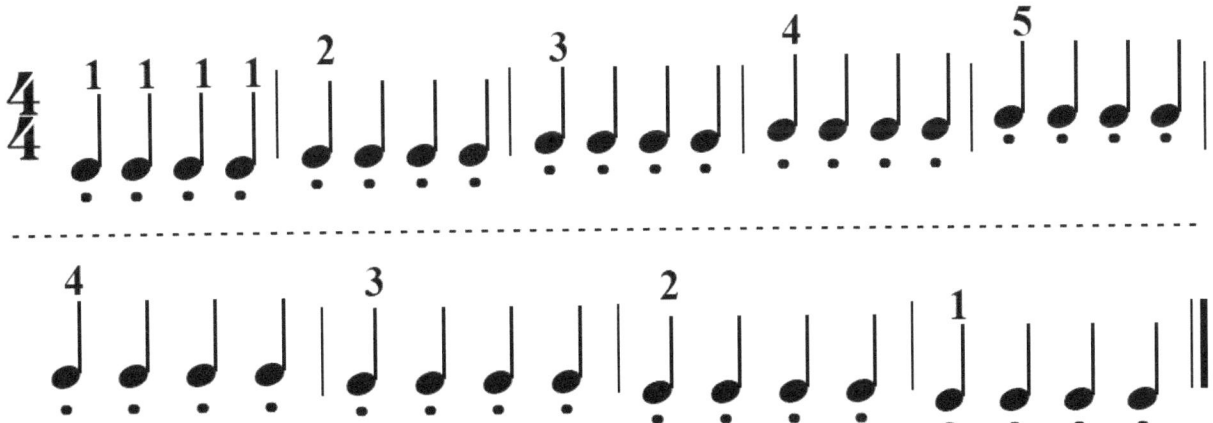

Exercise 13. Teeter Totter L.H.

Practicing rocking the wrist

1. Clap and count the rhythm.
2. Lift your hand and gently rock your wrist side to side.
3. First, tap this exercise on the piano lid while counting. Use the rocking motion.
4. Next, play it on the keyboard and count out loud. Play the entire exercise *legato*.
5. Check that your longer fingers — 2, 3, and 4 — are above the three black keys.

Home

Exercise 14. Teeter Totter R.H.

Practicing rocking the wrist

1. Clap and count the rhythm.
2. Lift your hand and gently rock your wrist side to side.
3. First, tap this exercise on the piano lid while counting. Use the rocking motion.
4. Next, play it on the keyboard and count out loud. Play the entire exercise *legato*.
5. Check that your longer fingers — 2, 3, and 4 — are above the three black keys.

Home

Exercise 15. Kangaroo L.H.

Developing a flexible wrist

1. Clap the rhythm and count out loud.

2. Tap the exercise on the piano lid while you count. Pretend the kangaroo is jumping with both feet!

3. Now play it on the keyboard and keep counting as you play.

Home

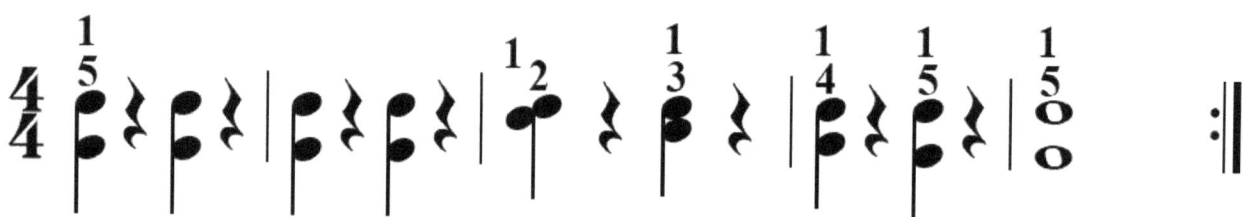

Exercise 16. Kangaroo R.H.

Developing a flexible wrist

1. Clap the rhythm and count out loud.

2. Tap the exercise on the piano lid while you count. Pretend the kangaroo is jumping with both feet!

3. Now play it on the keyboard and keep counting as you play.

Home

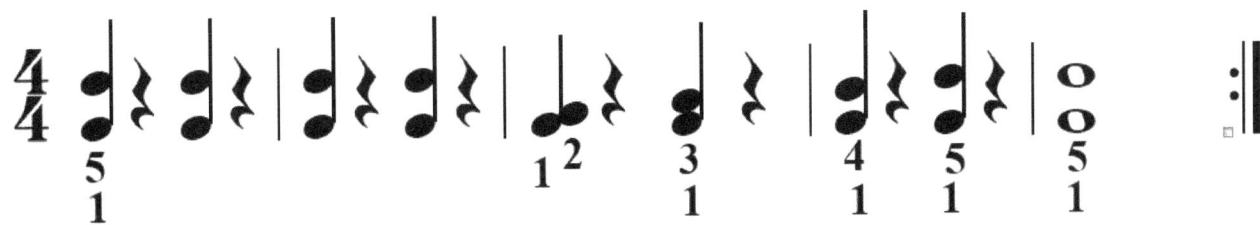

Exercise 17. Mama and Two Babies L.H.

Three notes per stroke

1. Clap the rhythm and count out loud.
2. Tap the rhythm on the piano lid using the correct finger numbers. Let the first note of each group fall with a gentle arm drop, then join the second and third notes.
3. Play the pattern on the keyboard. Connect the notes with a smooth *legato* and keep counting as you play.

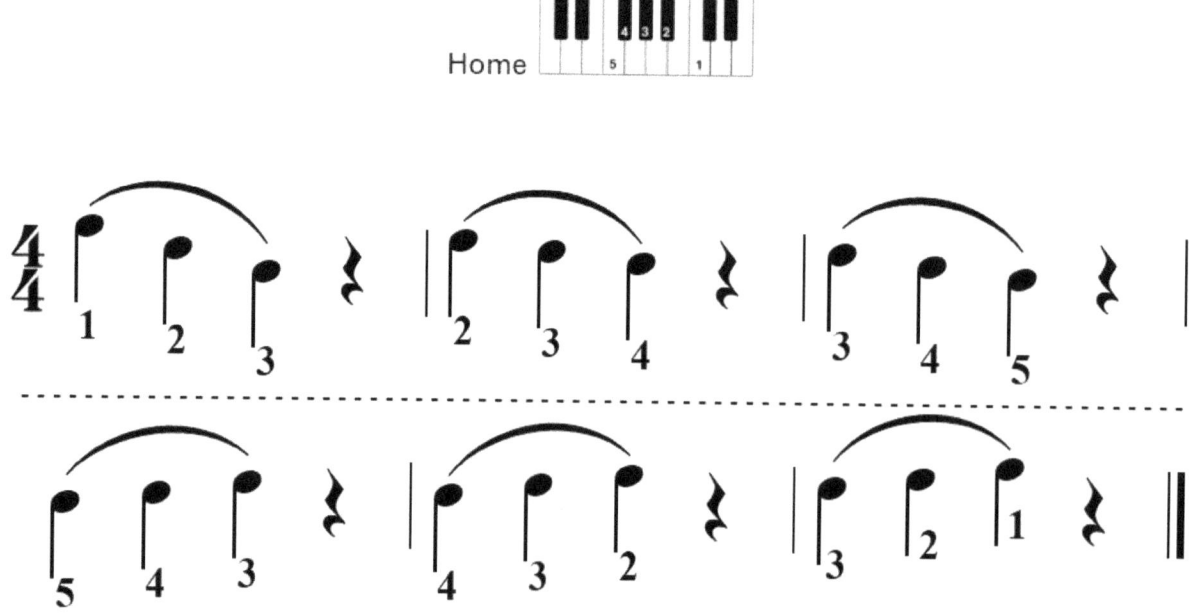

Exercise 18. Mama and Two Babies R.H.

Three notes per stroke

1. Clap the rhythm and count out loud.
2. Tap the rhythm on the piano lid using the correct finger numbers. Let the first note of each group fall with a gentle arm drop, then join the second and third notes.
3. Play the pattern on the keyboard. Connect the notes with a smooth *legato* and keep counting as you play.

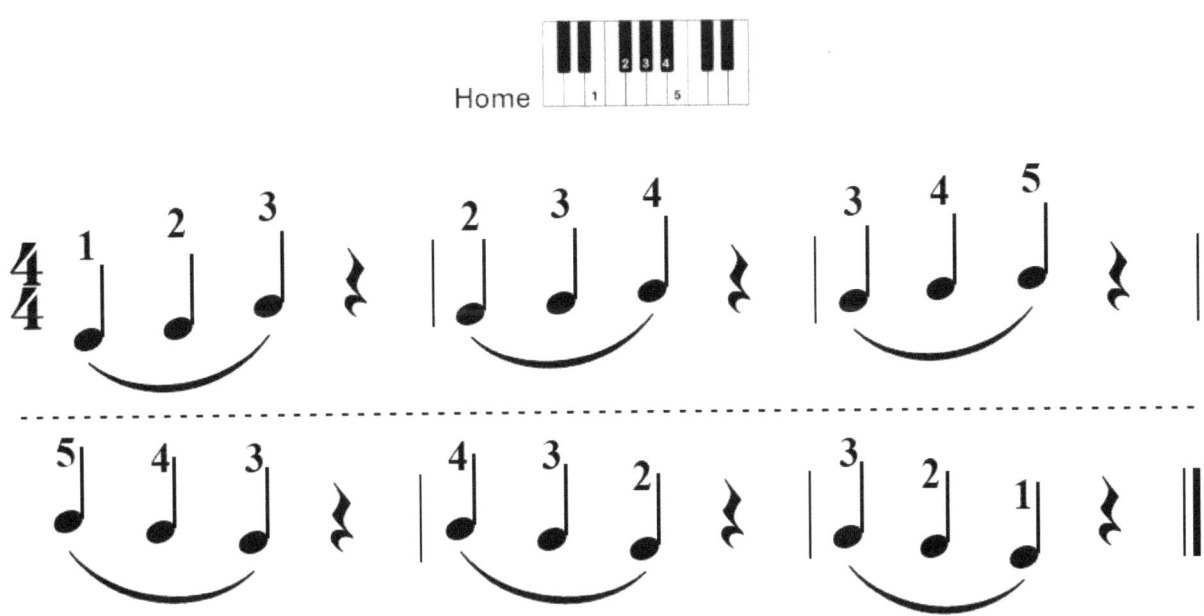

Exercise 19. A Marching Band L.H.

Developing a long legato

1. Clap the rhythm and count out loud.
2. Tap the rhythm on the piano lid using the correct finger numbers. Lift each finger slightly before playing, as if your fingers are marching.
3. Play the exercise on the keyboard. Connect the notes with a smooth *legato* and keep counting as you play.
4. Keep your wrist flat. It should stay steady and not bounce with every note.

Home

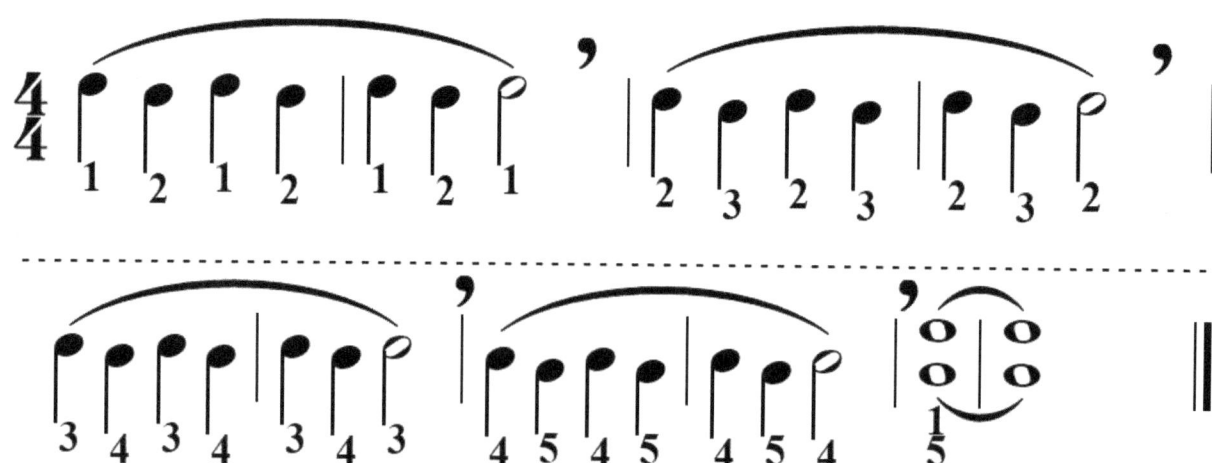

Exercise 20. A Marching Band R.H.

Developing a long legato

1. Clap the rhythm and count out loud.

2. Tap the rhythm on the piano lid using the correct finger numbers. Lift each finger slightly before playing, as if your fingers are marching.

3. Play the exercise on the keyboard. Connect the notes with a smooth *legato* and keep counting as you play.

4. Keep your wrist flat. It should stay steady and not bounce with every note.

Home

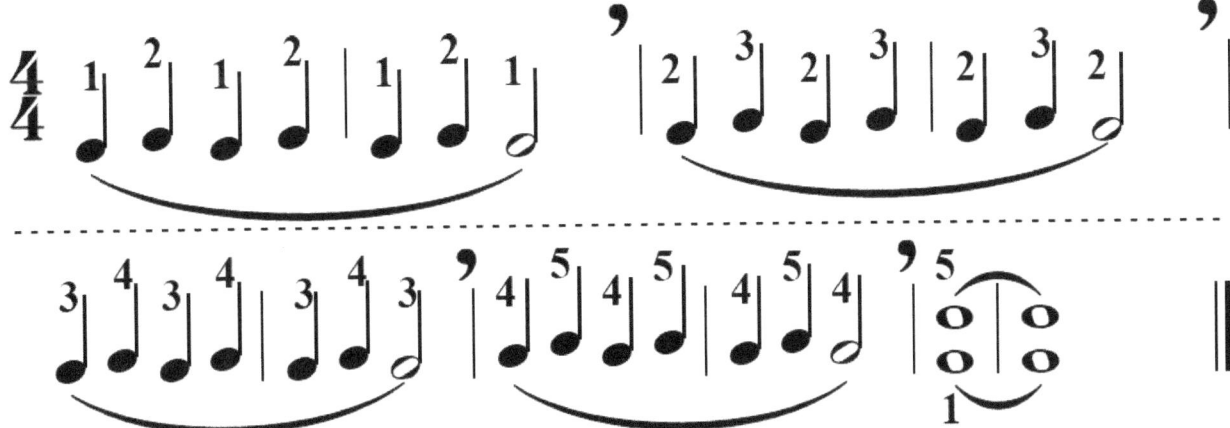

Exercise 21. Jump-Rope L.H.

Legato and staccato combo

1. Clap the rhythm and count out loud.
2. Tap the exercise on the piano lid while counting out loud. Connect the first note to the second with a smooth ***legato***, then lift off the key with a light, clean jump.
3. Now play it on the keyboard and keep counting as you play.

Home

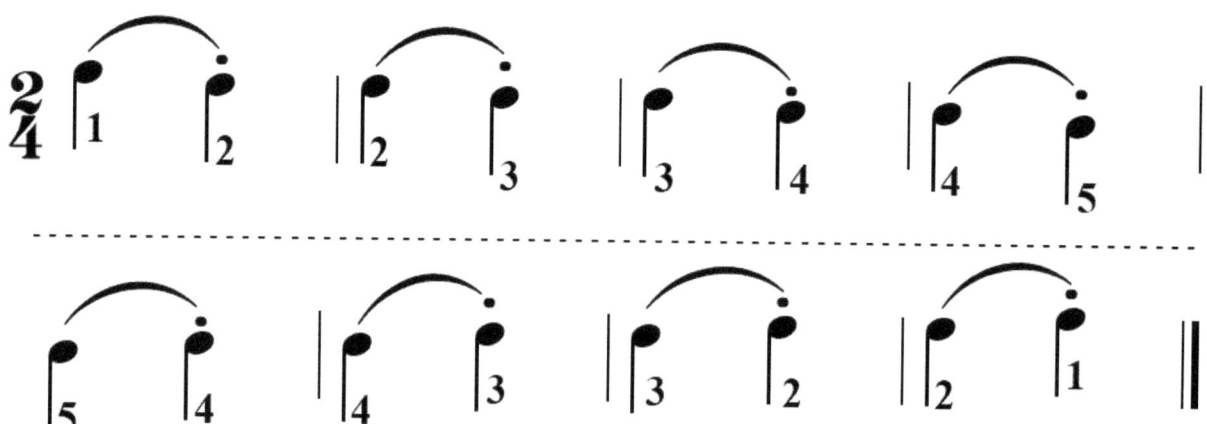

Exercise 22. Jump-Rope R.H.

Legato and staccato combo

1. Clap the rhythm and count out loud.
2. Tap the exercise on the piano lid while counting out loud. Connect the first note to the second with a smooth *legato*, then lift off the key with a light, clean jump.
3. Now play it on the keyboard and keep counting as you play.

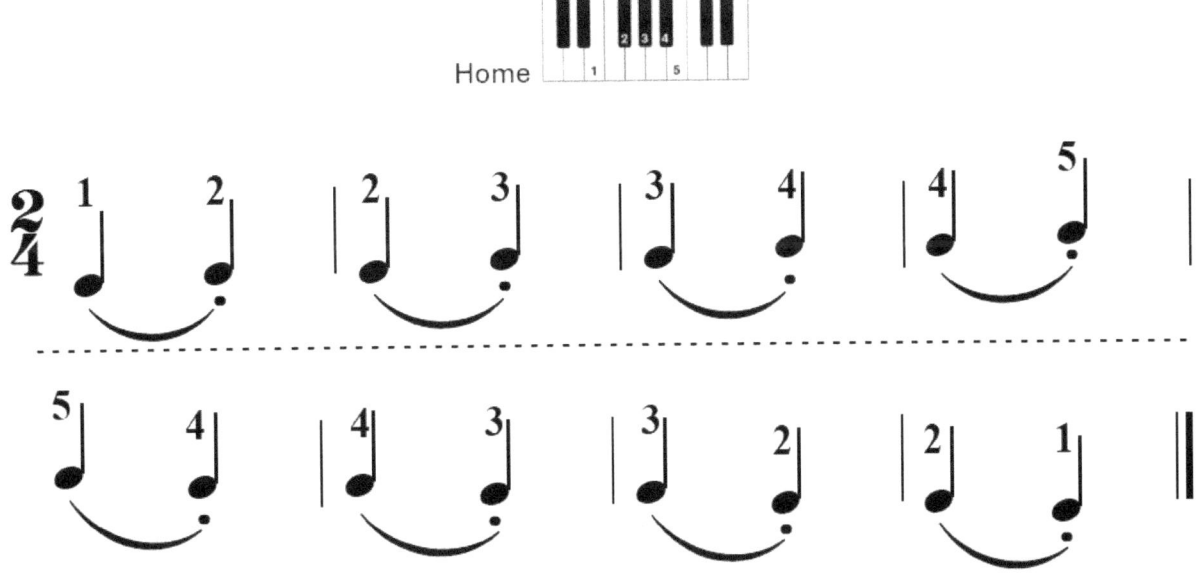

Exercise 23. On the Swing L.H.

Practicing four notes per stroke

1. Tap the rhythm on the piano lid while counting aloud. Play the first of the four notes with a gentle arm drop. Let the wrist roll slightly forward, connecting the four quarter notes as if you are pushing a swing and flying forward. Do the same motion for the backward "flight."
2. Maintain a good legato within each motive; do not strike the keys.
3. Now play the exercise on the keyboard, continuing to count as you play.
4. Keep your fingers naturally curved.

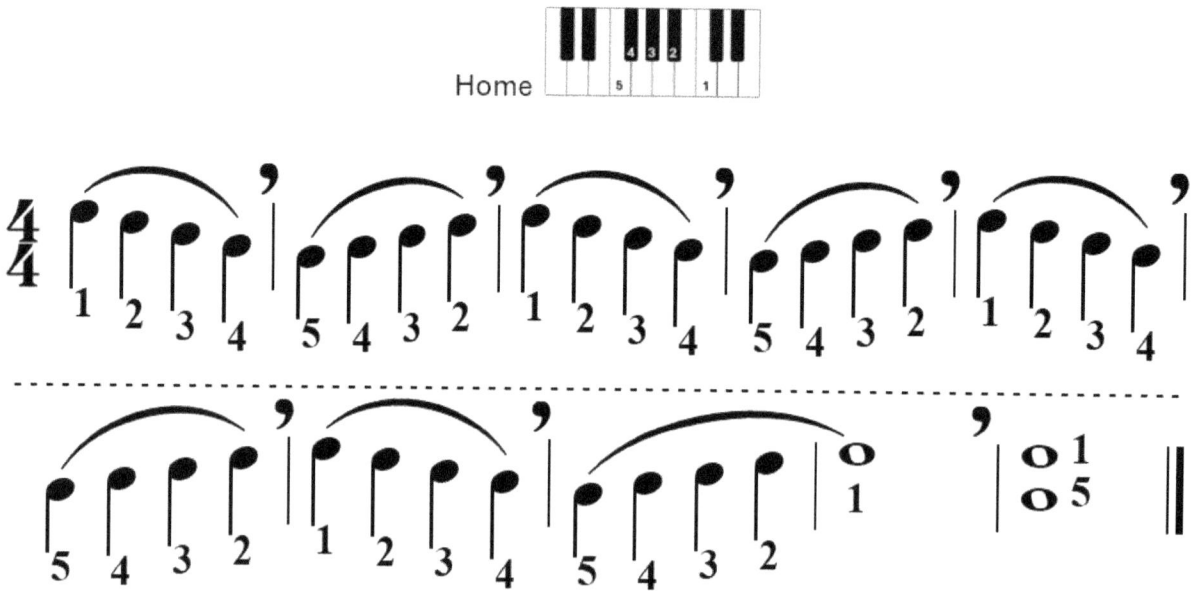

Exercise 24. On the Swing R.H.

Practicing four notes per stroke

1. Tap the rhythm on the piano lid while counting aloud. Play the first of the four notes with a gentle arm drop. Let the wrist roll slightly forward, connecting the four quarter notes as if you are pushing a swing and flying forward. Do the same motion for the backward "flight."

2. Maintain a good legato within each motive; do not strike the keys.

3. Now play the exercise on the keyboard, continuing to count as you play.

4. Keep your fingers naturally curved.

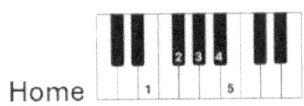

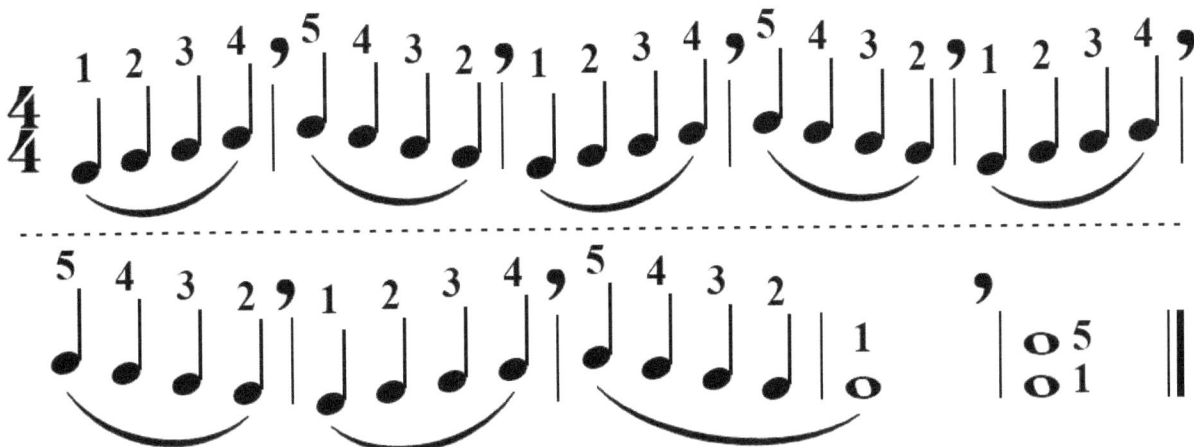

Exercise 25. Train L.H.

Maintaining a long legato

1. Play at a moderate tempo, counting aloud and maintaining a smooth *legato*.
2. Do not bounce your wrist while playing.
3. Keep your fingers gently curved.

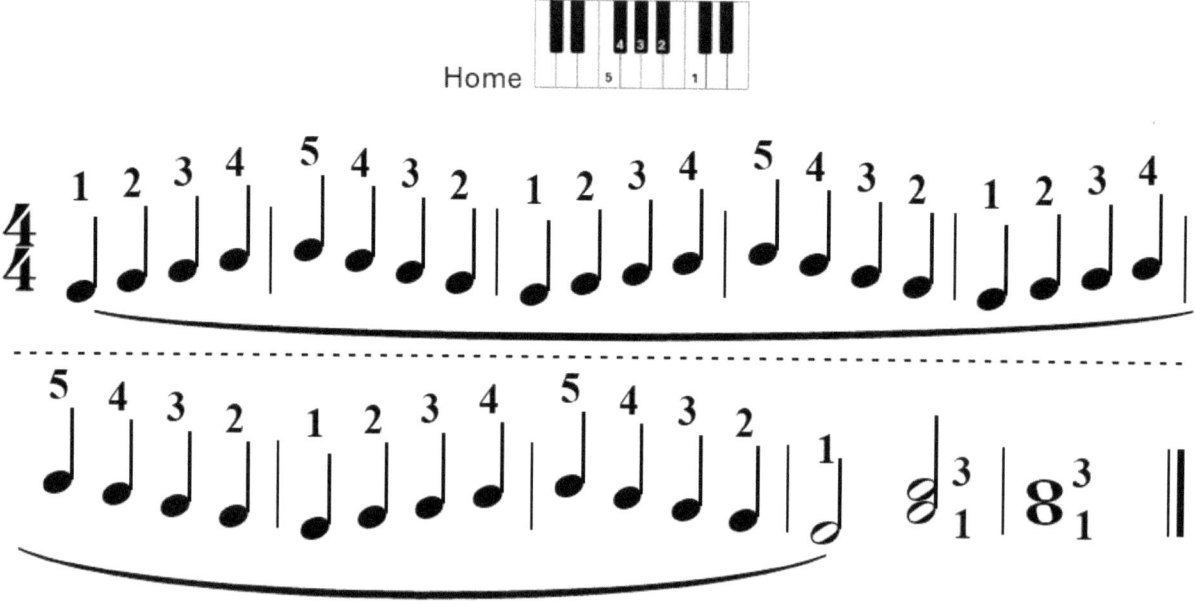

Exercise 26. Train R.H.

Maintaining a long legato

1. Play at a moderate tempo, counting aloud and maintaining a smooth *legato*.
2. Do not bounce your wrist while playing.
3. Keep your fingers gently curved.

Home

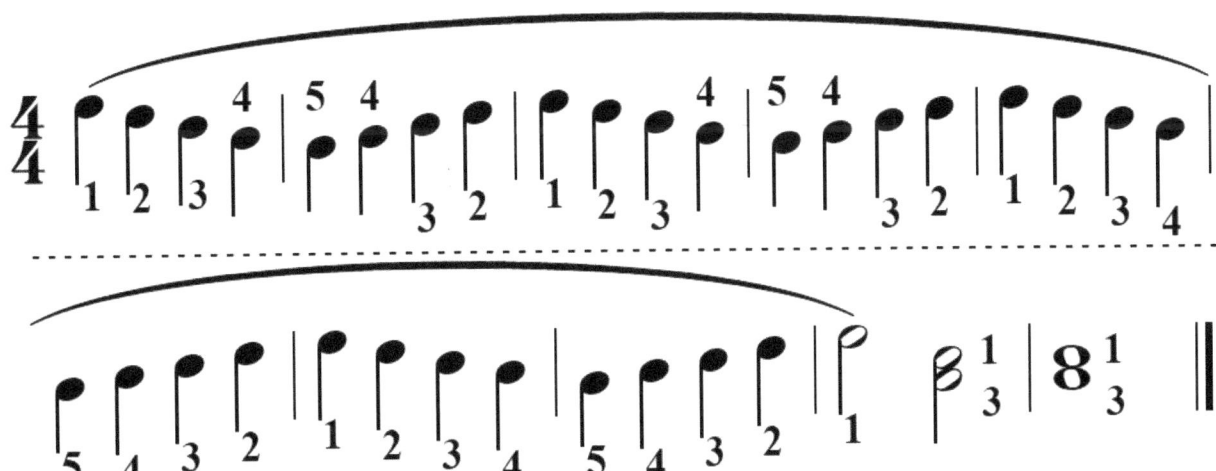

Exercise 27. Forest Woodpeckers L.H.

Playing Two Voices in One Hand

1. A short curved line, *a tie*, connecting the same notes tells you to hold the sound through five measures. While one finger holds the tied whole notes, the other plays short staccato notes, like a woodpecker. Then switch fingers.
2. Tap the exercise on the piano lid and count aloud. Use a gentle wrist-rocking motion to reduce tension.
3. Play the exercise on the keyboard, continuing to count as you play.

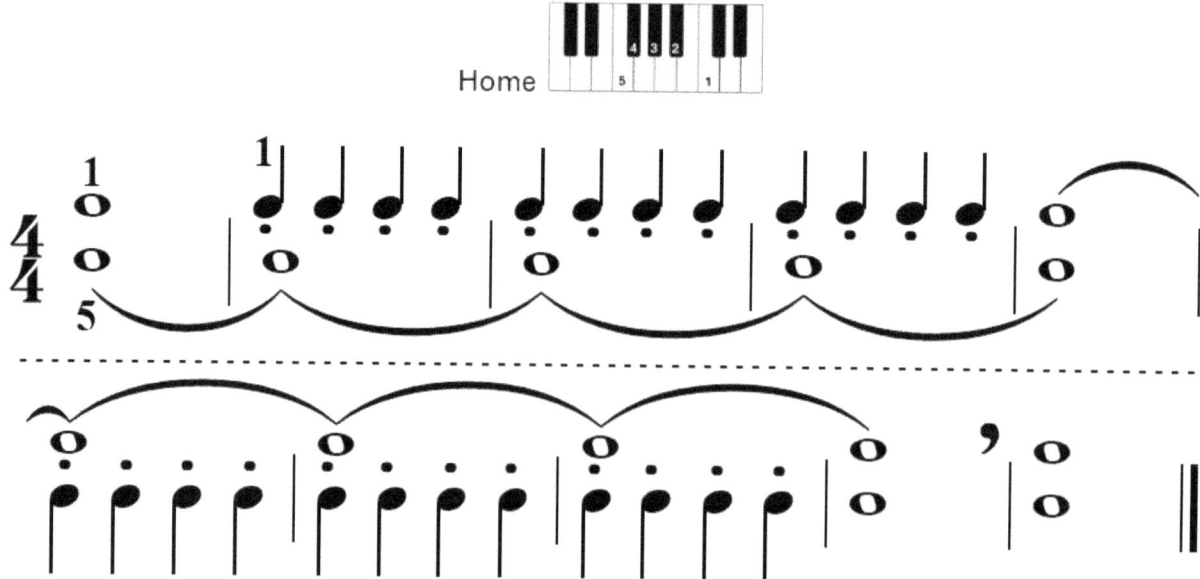

Exercise 28. Forest Woodpeckers R.H.

Playing Two Voices in One Hand

1. A short curved line, *a tie,* connecting the same notes tells you to hold the sound through five measures. While one finger holds the tied whole notes, the other plays short staccato notes, like a woodpecker.

   Then switch fingers.

2. Tap the exercise on the piano lid and count aloud. Use a gentle wrist-rocking motion to reduce tension.

3. Play the exercise on the keyboard, continuing to count as you play.

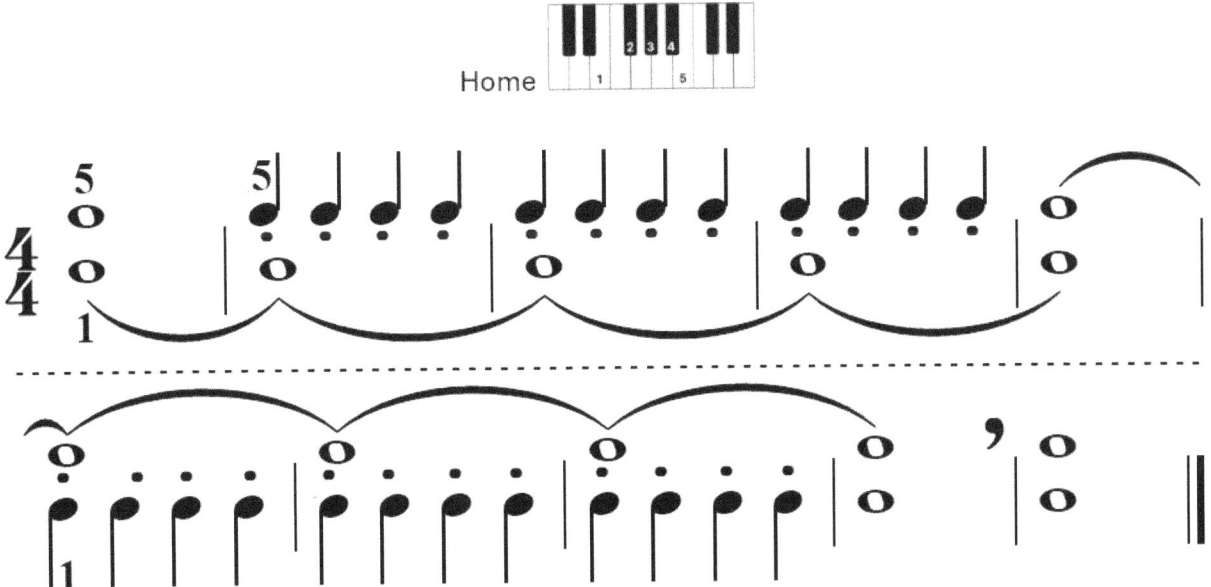

Exercise 29. Tribal Drum L.H.

Finger Independence

1. There are two voices in this exercise
2. Tap the whole notes on the piano lid and count. Lift your hand quickly on the breath marks.
3. Add the second voice (quarter notes). Play them with a slight pounding motion like the drum.
4. Play it on the piano.

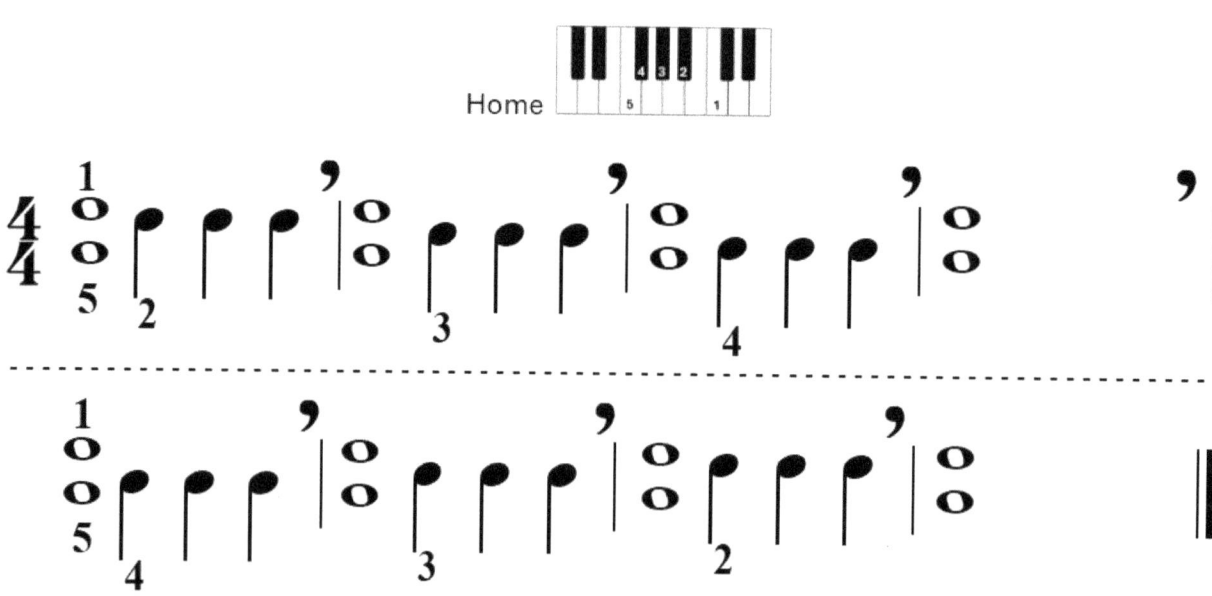

Exercise 30. Tribal Drum R.H.

Finger Independence

1. There are two voices in this exercise

2. Tap the whole notes on the piano lid and count. Lift your hand quickly on the breath marks.

3. Add the second voice (quarter notes). Play them with a slight pounding motion like the drum.

4. Play it on the piano.

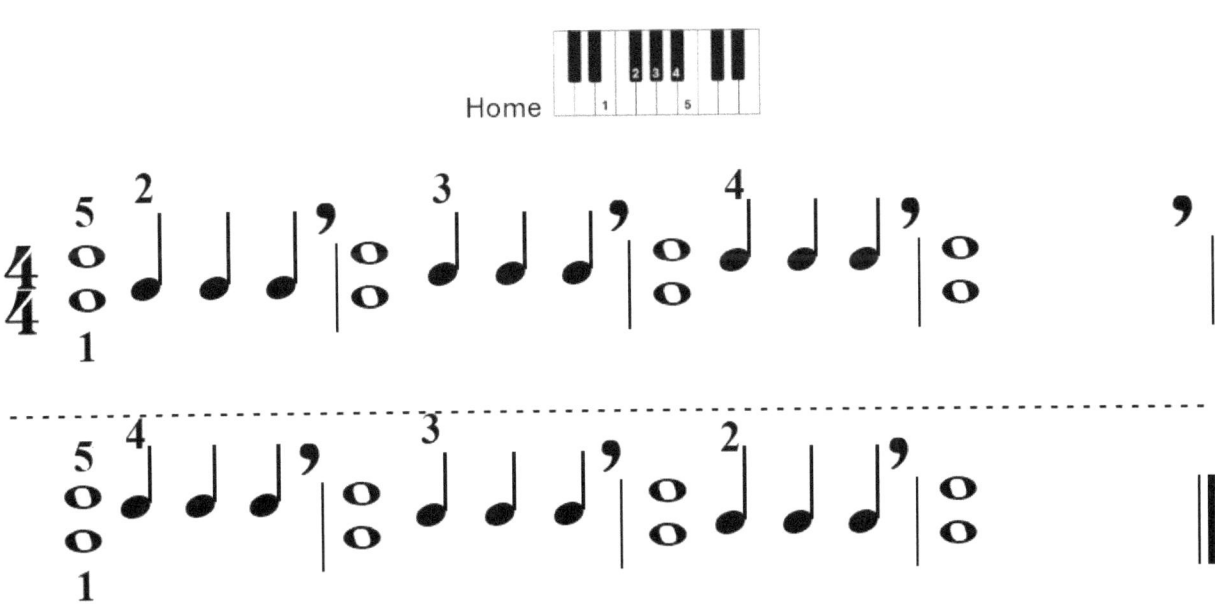

Exercise 31. Young Carpenter   L.H.

Finger Independence

1. Try this exercise on the piano lid, first.
2. Hold the whole notes to their full value
3. Smoothly connect them to the next pair of notes
4. Play the repeated quarter notes using a gentle pounding motion, like tapping with a hammer.

Home

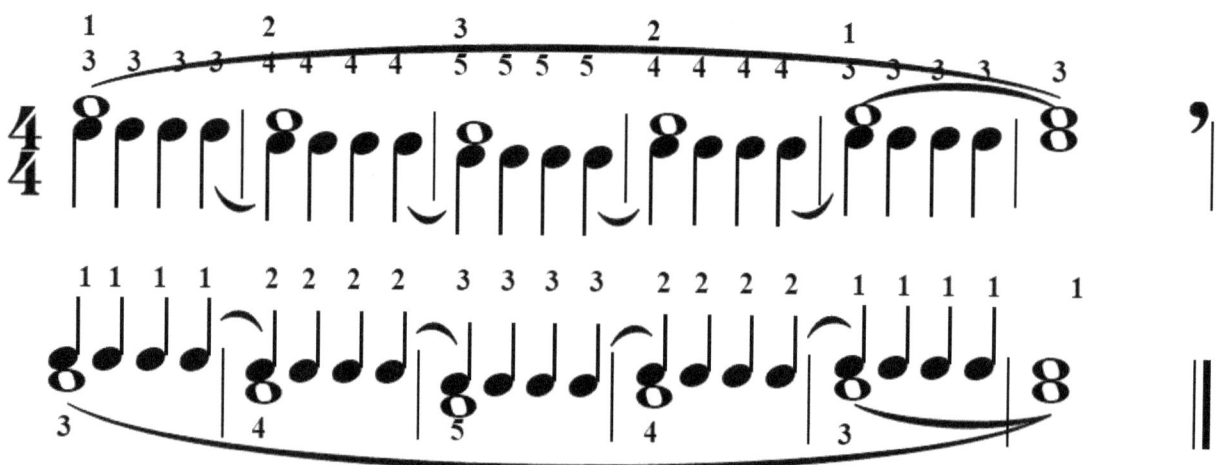

Exercise 32. Young Carpenter R.H.

Finger Independence

5. Try this exercise on the piano lid, first.

6. Hold the whole notes to their full value

7. Smoothly connect them to the next pair of notes

8. Play the repeated quarter notes using a gentle pounding motion, like tapping with a hammer.

Home

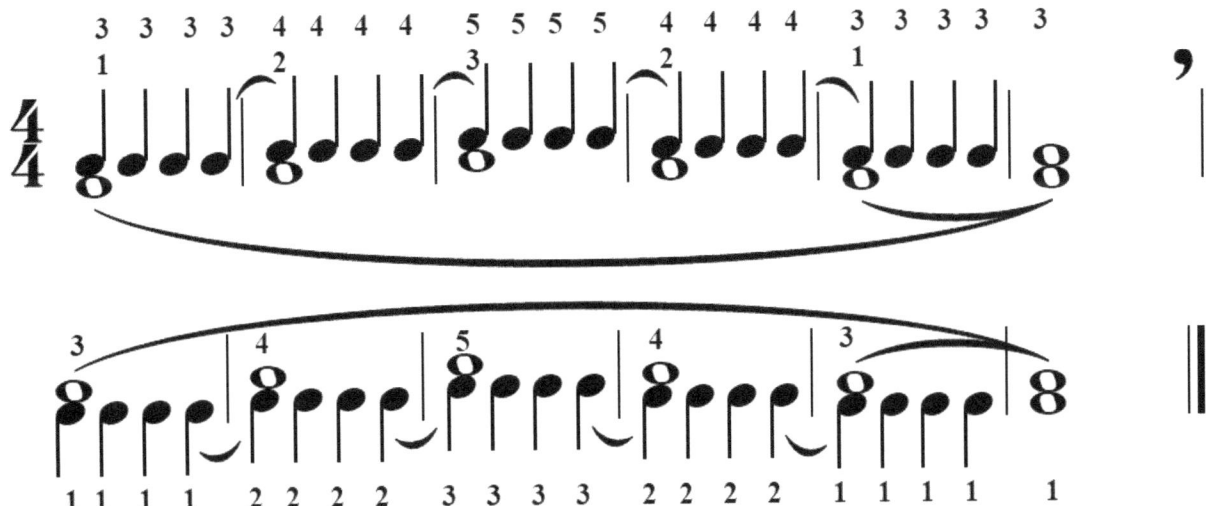

Exercise 33. Rainy Day L.H.

Practicing Chords

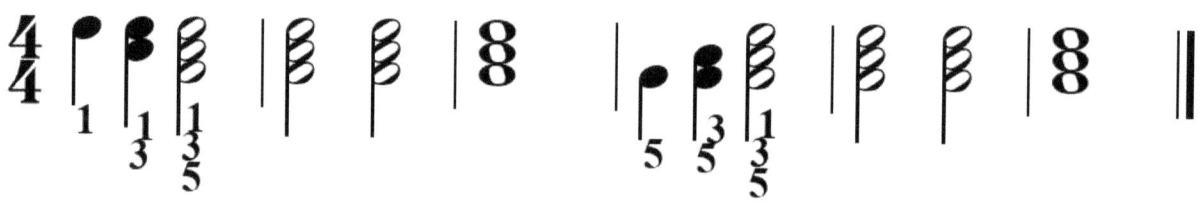

1. When we play three notes together, we call it *a chord*.
2. Tap on the piano lid and count.
3. Then play it on the piano.
4. Listen to how beautiful the chords sound.

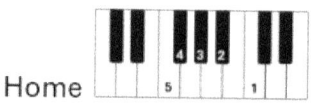

Home

Exercise 34. Sunny Day R.H.

Practicing Chords

1. When we play three notes together, we call it *a chord*.
2. Tap on the piano lid and count.
3. Then play it on the piano.
4. Listen to how beautiful the chords sound.

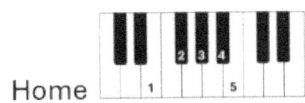

Home

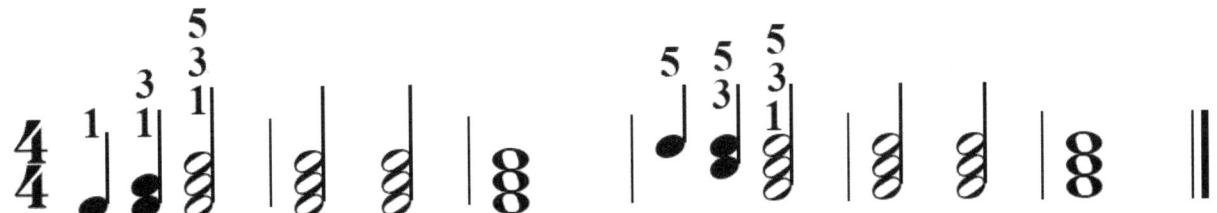

Exercise 35. Rock Climber L.H.

Two-Voice Legato in One Hand

This exercise is challenging.

The teacher may guide the student's eyes and hand to help feel the movement.

1. Here, two voices are singing together. Start with the first line.
2. First, learn the bottom voice (half notes). Play with good *legato* and hold each note for its full value.
3. Next, learn the top voice (whole notes). Maintain good *legato* and hold the notes for their full value.
4. Finally, play both voices together.
5. Do the same with the second line.
6. Now you can play the whole thing!

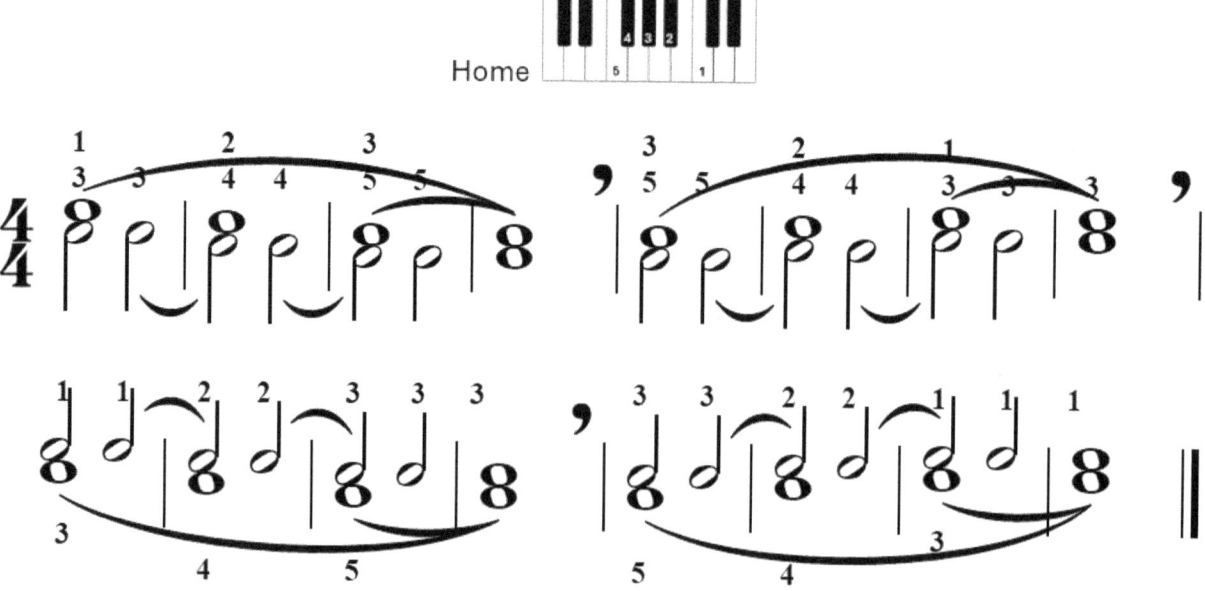

Exercise 36. Rock Climber R.H.

Two-Voice Legato in One Hand

This exercise is challenging.

The teacher may guide the student's eyes and hand to help feel the movement.

1. Here, two voices are singing together. Start with the first line.
2. First, learn the top voice (half notes). Play with good *legato* and hold each note for its full value.
3. Next, learn the bottom voice (whole notes). Maintain good *legato* and hold the notes for their full value.
4. Finally, play both voices together.
5. Do the same with the second line.
6. Now you can play the whole thing!

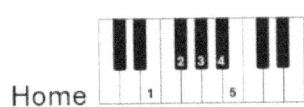

Home

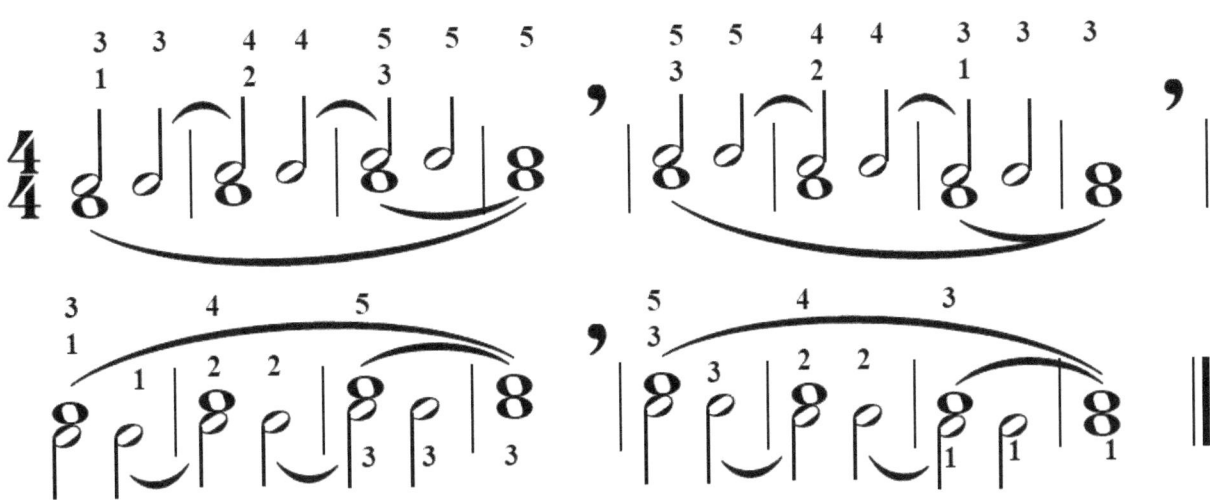

Exercise 37. The Sneaky Thumb L.H.

Thumb-Under Preparation for Scales

In this exercise, we do not use finger 5.

The thumb slips under the long fingers and plays again.

It is called *passing the thumb*.

Look at the chart below.

You will see finger 1 two times.

The thumb is playing hide-and-seek!

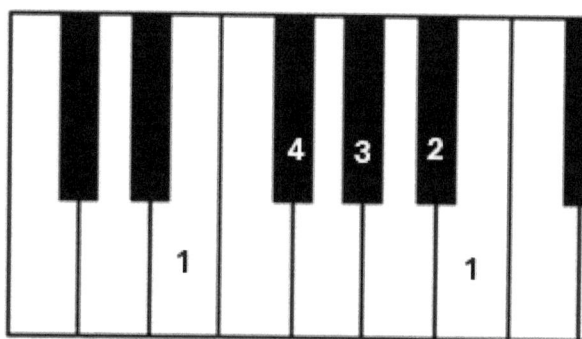

legato

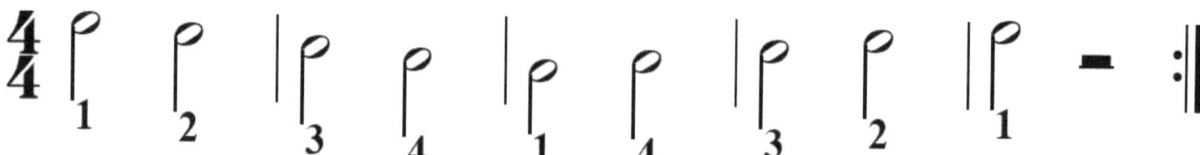

Exercise 38. The Sneaky Thumb R.H.

Thumb-Under Preparation for Scales

In this exercise, we do not use finger 5.

The thumb slips under the long fingers and plays again.

It is called *passing the thumb*.

Look at the chart below.

You will see finger 1 two times.

The thumb is playing hide-and-seek!

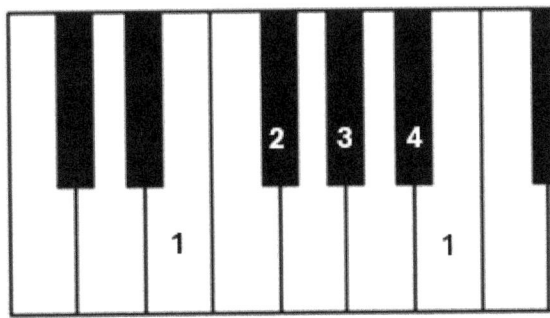

legato

Exercise 39. My First Scale Prep L.H.

B Major

The word *Scale* comes from the Italian word *"la scala"*, which means

a staircase.

When you play a scale, you climb the notes step by step — just like going up and down the stairs.

Your hand position will change here. First, your hand rests on three black keys.

Then it moves down to two black keys.

Let your hand travel gently along the keyboard.

These are *clusters:*

When notes share one stem, they are played together.

Here you see two kinds of clusters: two notes together (two black keys) and three notes together (three black keys).

Clusters sound different from other chords and are fun to play!

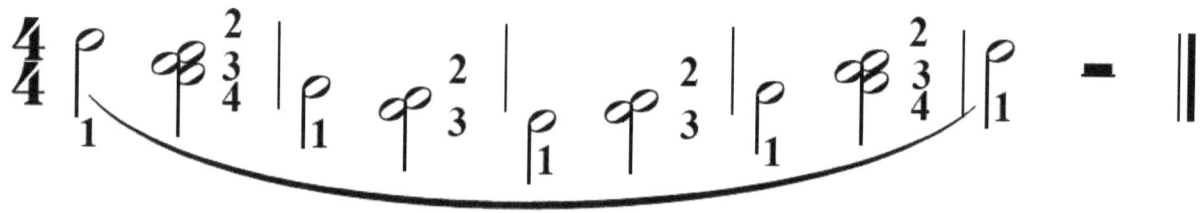

Exercise 40. My First Scale Prep R.H.

B Major

Your hand position will change here.

First, your hand rests on three black keys. Then it moves to two black keys.

Let your hand travel gently along the keyboard.

These are *clusters:*

When notes share one stem, they are played together.

Here you see two kinds of clusters: two notes together (two black keys) and three notes together (three black keys).

Clusters sound different from other chords and are fun to play!

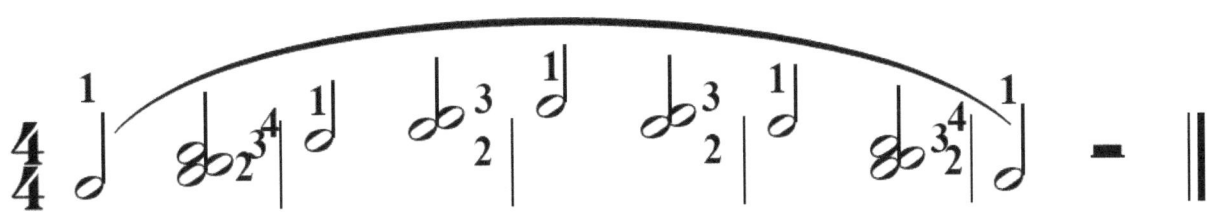

B Major Scale L.H.

In the B Major scale, only two keys are white: B and E.

Play them with finger 1.

The black keys are played with fingers 2, 3, and 4.

Copy the finger numbers from the circles.

Then play the scale up and down.

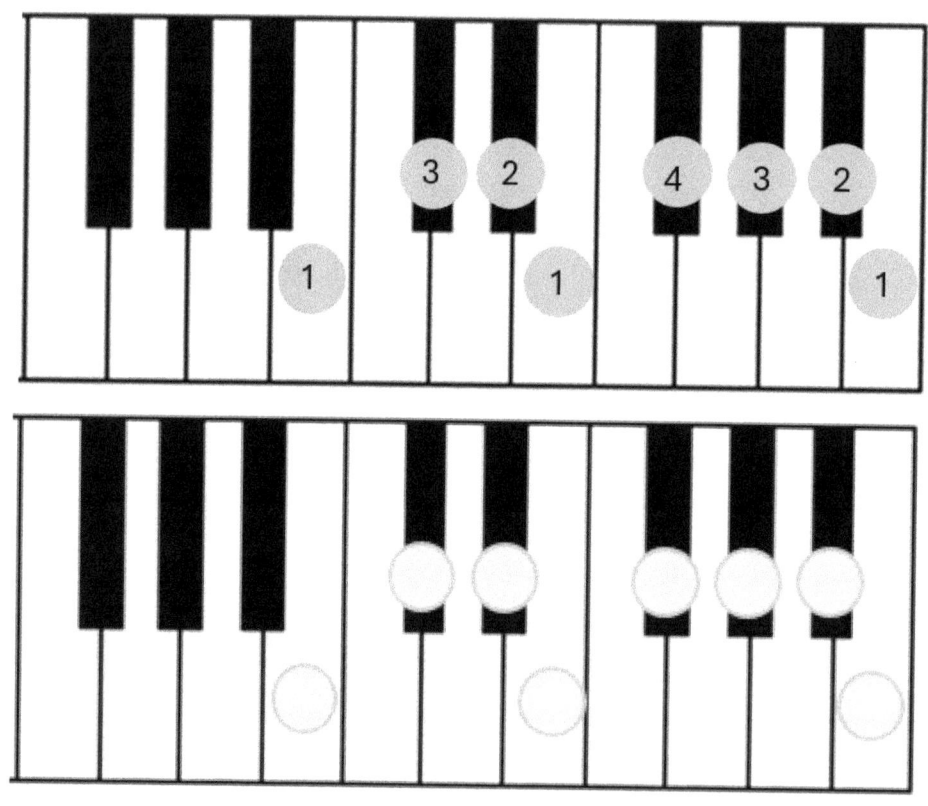

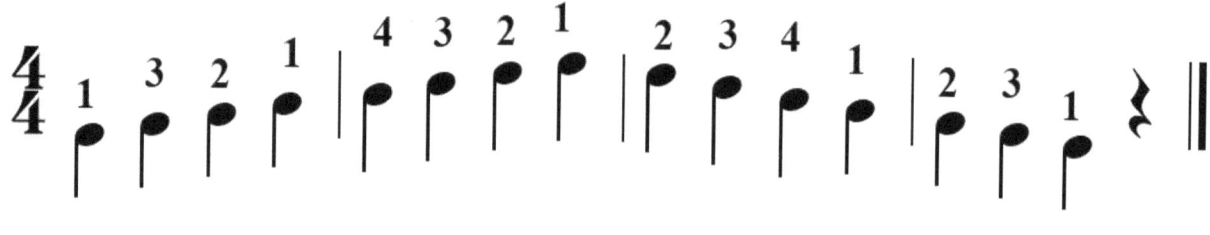

legato

B Major Scale R.H.

In the B Major scale, only two keys are white: B and E.

Play them with finger 1.

The black keys are played with fingers 2, 3, and 4.

Copy the finger numbers from the circles.

Then play the scale up and down.

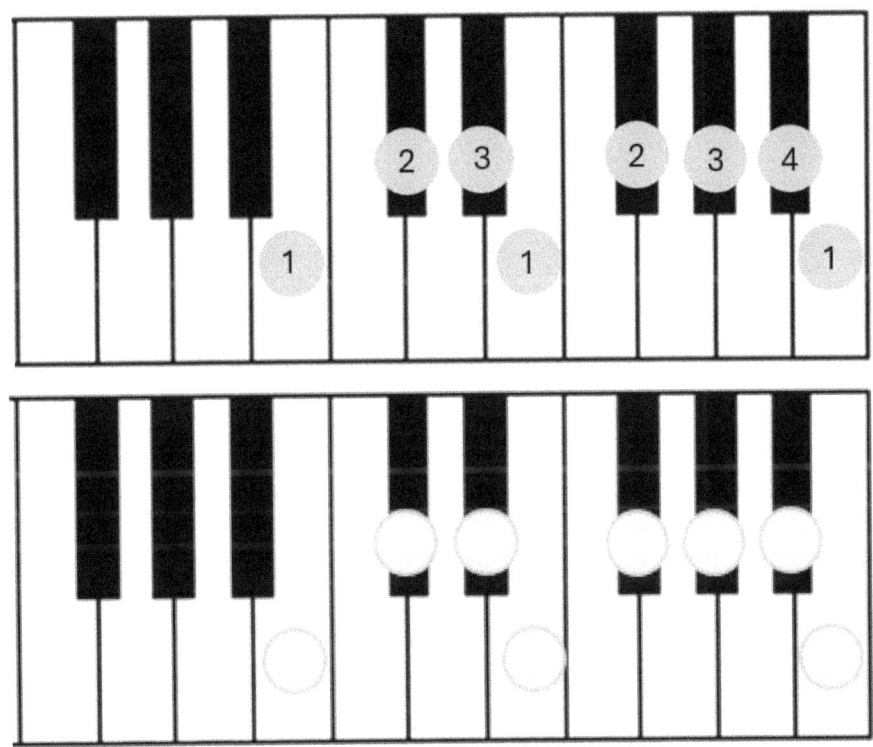

legato

Flight of the Tiny Bumblebee L. H.

Three -Black-Key Chromatic Prep

1. This exercise prepares the hand for the *chromatic scale*. It is played on three black keys and the two white keys between them, using only fingers 1 and 3.

2. Look at the chart below: Finger 3 plays the black keys, and finger 1 plays the white keys. Keep your hand relaxed and imagine a little bumblebee flying lightly from key to key.

3. Play slowly at first, listening for evenness and a smooth, flowing motion. Speed may increase naturally once the movement feels easy and comfortable.

Flight of the Tiny Bumblebee R.H.

Three-Black-Key Chromatic Prep

1. This exercise prepares the hand for the *chromatic scale*. It is played on three black keys and the two white keys between them, using only fingers 1 and 3.

2. Look at the chart below: Finger 3 plays the black keys, and finger 1 plays the white keys. Keep your hand relaxed and imagine a little bumblebee flying lightly from key to key.

3. Play slowly at first, listening for evenness and a smooth, flowing motion. Speed may increase naturally once the movement feels easy and comfortable.

Chromatic Scale L. H.

Chromatic scale — a scale that moves by half steps, using all the black and white keys in order.

This scale is played with **three fingers only: 1, 2, and 3**.

Look at the chart below: the **black keys** are played with **finger 3**; the **white keys** are played with **finger 1**, except when **two white keys are next to each other** — they are played with **fingers 1 and 2**.

When you master this pattern, you can travel across the entire keyboard with this amazing sound!   Play it *legato*.

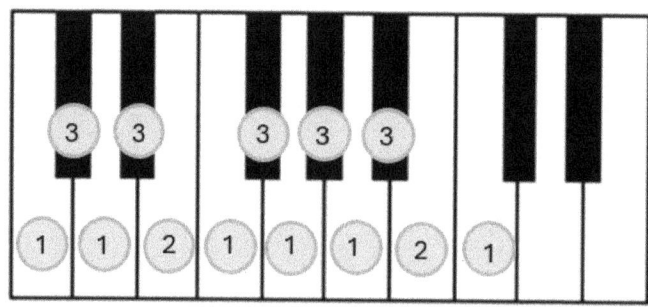

Chromatic Scale R. H.

Chromatic scale — a scale that moves by half steps, using all the black and white keys in order.

This scale is played with **three fingers only: 1, 2, and 3.**

Look at the chart below: the **black keys** are played with **finger 3**; the **white keys** are played with **finger 1**, except when **two white keys are next to each other** — they are played with **fingers 1 and 2**.

When you master this pattern, you can travel across the entire keyboard with this amazing sound! Play it *legato*.

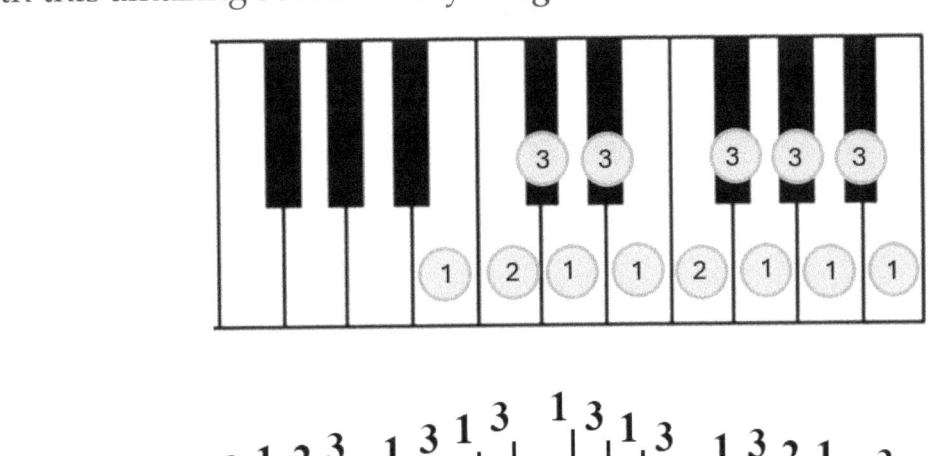

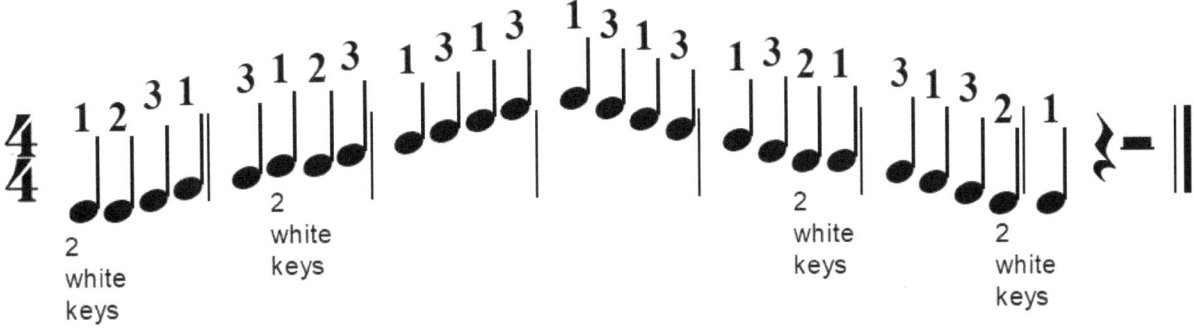

MUSIC PAPER

Teacher's Guide

Purpose of This Book

Skillful Little Fingers, Book I, is designed to prepare the beginner's hand for healthy, natural piano playing.

Its primary goal is not speed, early repertoire, or fast results, but the development of balance, freedom, coordination, and listening.

This book focuses on **how the hand moves**, not just on which notes are played.

Many technical difficulties in later piano study arise not from lack of talent, but from tension formed at the very beginning. For this reason, the exercises in this book are carefully sequenced to build coordination **before** introducing complex demands such as scales, fast passages, or hand crossings.

From the first pages, the student is guided to experience:

- stability without stiffness,
- movement without force,
- independence without tension.

The hand learns to feel weight, direction, and connection through simple patterns and precise physical gestures. Musical elements such as legato, staccato, voicing, and two-note balance are introduced early, but always through **movement and listening**, rather than through mechanical drilling.

This book also places strong emphasis on **preparation away from the keyboard**. Tapping exercises on the piano lid allow students to explore rhythm, motion, and coordination without the added complexity of pitch. This approach helps prevent tension and supports confident transfer to the keyboard.

Imagery plays a central role throughout the book. Swings, woodpeckers, drums, climbers, and stairs are not decorative illustrations; they serve as physical metaphors that help young students understand motion, balance, and direction naturally and memorably.

By the end of Book I, the student is not merely "ready to play a scale," but is physically and musically prepared to do so. The introduction of the B Major scale is the result of accumulated experience, not a sudden technical challenge.

This book is intended to be used flexibly and thoughtfully. Progress is measured not by tempo or the number of completed exercises, but by the quality of movement, sound, and ease.

How to Use This Book

This book is designed to be used **slowly, flexibly, and thoughtfully**.
It is not necessary to complete one exercise per lesson, nor is it expected that students progress through the book at a fixed pace.

The order of exercises is intentional and should generally be respected. Each exercise prepares a specific physical or musical skill required for the next. However, the time spent on each exercise may vary substantially from student to student.

Some students may require several lessons to feel comfortable with a single pattern, whereas others may progress more quickly. Both approaches are valid.

Teachers are encouraged to:

- revisit earlier exercises whenever needed,
- alternate between familiar and new material,
- and allow repetition without pressure.

This book is not meant to replace repertoire, but to **support it**. Exercises may be used:

- at the beginning of the lesson to prepare the hand,
- as short technical work between pieces,
- or selectively, focusing only on specific challenges the student is facing.

Many exercises begin **away from the keyboard**, on the piano lid. This is an essential part of the method. Tapping helps students focus on rhythm, motion, and coordination without the distraction of pitch. Teachers should allow time for this step and avoid rushing to the keys.

Teacher guidance is expected and encouraged, especially in more advanced or "threshold" exercises. Guiding the student's hand, demonstrating motion, or helping the student follow the notes visually are not signs of weakness. It is a normal and healthy part of learning new physical skills.

Progress should be evaluated not by speed or accuracy alone, but by:

- freedom of movement,

- absence of tension,
- quality of sound,
- and the student's ability to listen and adjust.

If an exercise feels unstable or uncomfortable, it is appropriate to pause, return to earlier material, or simplify the task. The goal is always ease and clarity, not endurance.

This book may be used with students of different ages, but the language and imagery are especially effective with young beginners. Teachers are encouraged to adapt explanations to the students' age while preserving the underlying physical ideas.

The Core Principles of the Method

The method presented in *Skillful Little Fingers* is built on a small number of clear and consistent principles. These principles guide every exercise in the book and shape the way technique is introduced from the very beginning.

Early in the learning process, the student's hands become comfortable with both white and black keys, reducing fear and laying the groundwork for later theoretical study.

Movement Before Notes

The hand learns best through movement. Before focusing on pitch, speed, or reading, the student is guided to experience simple, natural motions: dropping, lifting, rolling, tapping, and balancing. Notes are introduced as part of these movements, not as isolated targets.

Freedom Before Control

Accurate control of the piano grows out of freedom, not tension. The method avoids prematurely forcing finger independence or strength. Instead, it first develops ease, weight awareness, and coordination. Control emerges naturally as the hand becomes more comfortable and balanced.

Whole-Arm Coordination

Finger movement is never isolated from the rest of the playing mechanism. From the earliest exercises, fingers, wrist, forearm, and arm work together as a coordinated unit. Even small movements are supported by the arm's larger structure, helping to prevent strain and stiffness.

Listening as a Technical Skill

Listening is treated as an essential part of the technique. Students are encouraged to notice differences in sound, length, connection, and balance from the very beginning. Musical awareness is developed alongside physical skill rather than added later.

Preparation Before Complexity

Every new technical element is prepared in advance. Before scales appear, the hand experiences:

- long notes and sustained balance,
- repeated notes and controlled motion,
- two voices within one hand,
- and gentle thumb-under preparation.

Nothing is introduced suddenly or without context.

Simplicity and Repetition

Exercises are intentionally short and simple. This allows students to repeat movements without fatigue and to focus on quality rather than quantity. Repetition is used to build confidence and familiarity, not to exert pressure.

Imagery as a Learning Tool

Physical images play a central role in the method. Swings, drums, woodpeckers, climbers, and stairs give students concrete references for abstract motions. These images help translate complex physical ideas into experiences that young students can easily understand and remember.

The Teacher as Guide

The teacher is an active guide throughout the learning process. Demonstration, physical guidance, and shared attention are essential tools. The method assumes a supportive teaching presence and encourages intervention when it helps the student feel movement more clearly.

Together, these principles create a learning environment in which techniques develop naturally, safely, and musically. The goal is not early virtuosity, but a strong physical and musical foundation that will support all future piano study.

Chopin's Position

Chopin's Position is introduced at the very beginning of *Skillful Little Fingers* because it offers the most natural and balanced hand shape for the young beginner.

In this position, the longer fingers (2, 3, and 4) rest on the black keys, while the thumb (1) and little finger (5) remain on the white keys. This alignment allows the hand to follow the keyboard's natural geometry and supports a comfortable, well-balanced hand position.

For young students, Chopin's Position provides several significant advantages:

- the hand feels stable without being stiff,
- the wrist remains free and flexible,
- the fingers naturally curve without force,
- and the thumb is placed in a relaxed, non-collapsing position.

Rather than asking the student to "make a shape," the teacher should gently and naturally guide the hand into this position. The goal is not to fix the hand in place, but to help the student *feel* balance and ease.

Teachers may observe that students often feel more immediately secure in this position, particularly those with small hands. The black keys provide clear tactile reference points, helping the student orient the hand without excessive visual effort.

Chopin's Position is not treated as a rigid rule, but as a **home position**—a place the hand can return to whenever balance or comfort is lost. As the book progresses, the hand gradually learns to move away from this position and travel along the keyboard, always maintaining the same sense of balance and freedom.

Throughout the book, Chopin's Position serves as a physical foundation. It supports finger independence, smooth legato, controlled articulation, and, later, the introduction of thumb-under motion and scales.

Teachers are encouraged to return to this position whenever tension appears. It remains a reliable point of reference not only for beginners but throughout the student's technical development.

Comfort on the Black Keys

A central goal of this book is to remove a child's fear of the black keys.
Long before learning sharps, flats, or the circle of fifths, the student's fingers develop ease and confidence across the entire keyboard.

Chromatic patterns move step by step through groups of keys, helping the student feel how black and white keys belong together. This prepares the hand for chromatic movement while building stability, coordination, and security on the black keys.

Through Chopin's Position, B major, and chromatic preparation, the black keys are presented as friendly, natural, and stable.
When music theory is introduced later, the hands already feel at home.

Working Away from the Keyboard

A distinctive feature of *Skillful Little Fingers* is the frequent use of exercises performed **away from the keyboard**, most often on the piano lid. This approach is intentional and serves several critical pedagogical purposes.

Working on the piano lid removes the complexity of pitch and allows the student to focus entirely on **movement, rhythm, and coordination**. Without the need to locate keys or worry about accuracy, the student can experience motion more freely and without tension.

These exercises help develop:

- a clear sense of pulse and timing,
- coordinated hand and arm movement,
- controlled lifting and dropping motions,
- and awareness of sound length through counting.

Tapping exercises also facilitate young students' understanding of musical gestures, such as legato, staccato, repeated notes, and grouped motion. The physical act of tapping mirrors the movement later used on the keyboard, creating a direct and natural transfer.

For many students, working away from the keys reduces anxiety. The piano lid serves as a neutral space in which exploration feels safe and playful. This is especially helpful when introducing new or challenging concepts, such as two voices in one hand or thumb-under preparation.

Teachers are encouraged to treat these exercises as a meaningful part of the lesson, not as a preliminary step to be rushed through. Time spent tapping is time spent building coordination and confidence.

When transferring an exercise from the lid to the keyboard, the teacher should emphasize that the **same movement** is being used. The keys simply add sound and pitch to a motion the student already understands physically.

If a student shows signs of tension or confusion at the keyboard, returning briefly to the piano lid can often restore clarity and ease. This back-and-forth between surface and keys supports steady, comfortable progress.

Working away from the keyboard reinforces the idea that technique is rooted in **movement and listening**, not in pressing keys. It prepares the student's hand and body for healthy playing long before technical demands increase.

Rhythm, Weight, and Natural Arm Motion

In *Skillful Little Fingers*, rhythm is introduced not only as a counting skill but as a **physical experience**. From the earliest exercises, rhythm is connected to motion, weight, and timing in the body.

Young students naturally understand rhythm through movement. Tapping, lifting, dropping, and rocking motions help them feel the pulse and duration before they are asked to control sound on the keys. This physical grounding makes rhythmic accuracy more stable and prevents rigid or forced playing.

Weight is introduced through gentle arm drop motions rather than finger pressure. Students learn to allow the arm's natural weight to produce sound, thereby avoiding tension in the fingers and wrist. Even light sounds are supported by the arm, creating a fuller, more relaxed tone.

The wrist plays a central role in coordinating motion. Small, flexible wrist movements—such as rolling forward, rocking, or releasing—help connect notes smoothly and support both legato and articulation. The wrist is never held stiffly, nor is it exaggerated; it remains responsive and free.

Repeated notes and grouped patterns are taught through **coordinated motion** rather than isolated finger action. Exercises that use pounding, tapping, or bouncing images encourage students to perceive a single gesture rather than a series of disconnected movements.

Teachers should carefully observe the student's arm and shoulder. Signs of healthy motion include:

- relaxed shoulders,
- a freely moving wrist,
- fingers that respond rather than press,
- and sound that feels easy to produce.

Counting aloud is encouraged throughout the book. Counting helps the student coordinate motion with time and reinforces the connection between rhythm and movement. Breath marks further support natural phrasing and timely release of the hand.

By integrating rhythm, weight, and natural arm motion from the beginning, the method builds a technical foundation that supports clarity, endurance, and musical expression. As technical demands increase later, these early experiences allow the student to respond with ease rather than effort.

Finger Independence Without Tension

Finger independence is often conflated with finger strength or finger isolation. In *Skillful Little Fingers*, independence is approached differently: it grows out of **balance, coordination, and freedom of movement**, not force.

From the earliest exercises, students experience how different fingers can move while others remain relaxed and stable. This is first explored through simple patterns, long notes held against shorter ones, and repeated notes supported by the hand and arm.

Rather than asking the student to "hold fingers down," the method encourages the hand to **balance naturally**. When the arm and wrist support the hand well, the fingers can act independently without strain.

Exercises involving:

- held notes against moving notes,
- repeated notes in one finger,
- and simple two-voice textures,

introduce independence gradually and safely. These patterns allow the student to feel how one finger can move while another remains calm, without gripping or stiffening the hand.

Teachers should listen carefully for tension-related signs, such as:

- tightening of the wrist,
- lifting of the shoulder,
- collapsing of the thumb,
- or harsh, forced sound.

When tension arises, slowing the tempo, reducing the number of repetitions, or briefly returning to work on the piano lid can help restore ease.

Imagery plays a vital role in this process. Images such as woodpeckers, drums, and climbing encourage active fingers while reminding the student that the hand as a whole must remain balanced and secure.

It is important to remember that finger independence develops over time. The goal at this stage is not precision or speed, but **clarity of motion and comfort**. A relaxed, coordinated hand will naturally gain control and independence as experience grows.

By introducing finger independence in this way, the method prepares the student for more complex textures and technical demands without creating habits of tension that are difficult to undo later.

Two Voices in One Hand

Playing two voices within one hand is an essential step in the student's technical and musical development. In *Skillful Little Fingers*, this skill is introduced early, but in a carefully prepared and accessible way.

At this stage, two voices do not mean complexity or polyphonic thinking in the traditional sense. Instead, the student learns to distinguish between:

- a **moving voice** and a **sustained voice**,
- a **foreground sound** and a **background sound**,
- motion and balance within the same hand.

Exercises that combine long and short notes enable students to experience how one finger can remain calm and stable while another moves freely. This builds on earlier work in finger independence and reinforces balanced hand coordination.

The primary focus is not on volume control but on **clarity and awareness**. Students are encouraged to listen for:

- the continuity of the held notes,
- the smooth connection of moving notes,
- and the overall balance of sound within the hand.

Teachers should guide students to think of the two voices as "singing together." This image helps avoid mechanical playing and encourages musical listening from the beginning.

Teacher assistance is often helpful in these exercises. Guiding the student's eyes along the line of the held notes, or gently supporting the hand, can help the student understand the structure of the music and feel the coordination more clearly.

It is normal for these exercises to feel challenging at first. They represent a threshold in the student's development at which balance, listening, and coordination must work together. Patience and repetition are essential.

By introducing two voices in one hand at this early stage, the method prepares the student for more advanced textures found in scales, broken chords, and later repertoire. The student learns that complexity grows from clarity, not from effort.

The Role of Imagery and Metaphor

Imagery and metaphor play a central role in *Skillful Little Fingers*. They are not used as decoration or entertainment, but as **essential teaching tools** that help young students understand movement, coordination, and sound.

For beginners, abstract technical instructions are often difficult to grasp. Images translate complex physical ideas into experiences the child can feel, imagine, and remember. A swing explains wrist motion more clearly than technical terminology. A woodpecker describes repeated finger action more effectively than a mechanical explanation.

Each image in the book is chosen to support a specific physical or musical idea. For example:

- swings suggest smooth, continuous motion,
- drums suggest controlled, repeated sound supported by the arm,
- woodpeckers encourage active fingers without stiffness,
- stairs and ladders show direction and stepwise motion,
- climbers represent balance, risk, and careful coordination,
- hide-and-seek introduces the thumb-under motion playfully and without fear.

These metaphors help students internalize the technique naturally. Instead of focusing on what not to do, students are guided toward what the movement *feels like*. This reduces tension and increases confidence.

Imagery also supports memory. Children often recall a movement more easily through an image than through verbal instruction. When a student remembers "the swing" or "the climber," the physical motion returns quickly and naturally.

Teachers are encouraged to adapt the imagery to suit each student. Some children respond strongly to visual images, while others prefer physical demonstration or sound-based descriptions. The metaphors provided in the book are flexible tools, not rigid instructions.

Imagery must remain connected to physical reality. The teacher should consistently demonstrate the actual motion and help the student experience it physically. The image serves as a bridge between sensation and understanding.

By integrating imagery and metaphor throughout the method, *Skillful Little Fingers* creates a learning environment that is imaginative, grounded, and effective. Technique becomes something the student experiences as a whole-body experience, not something imposed from the outside.

Threshold Exercises

Some exercises in *Skillful Little Fingers* represent essential **thresholds** in the student's technical development. These are moments when previously learned skills must come together in novel ways. It is normal for these exercises to feel more challenging and to require additional time and guidance.

Threshold exercises often involve:

- balancing held notes against moving notes,
- coordinating two voices within one hand,
- maintaining legato while changing hand position,
- or introducing thumb-under motion for the first time.

Examples include exercises such as *Two Voices in One Hand*, *Rock Climber*, and *Hide-and-Seek*. These exercises ask the student to manage balance, coordination, and attention simultaneously. Difficulty at this stage does not indicate failure; it means growth.

Teachers should expect that students may:

- lose balance temporarily,
- slow down significantly,
- need frequent reminders to release tension,
- or require physical guidance.

All of these responses are normal.

During threshold exercises, the teacher's role is crucial. Guiding the student's hand, helping the student follow the notes visually, or modeling the motion through demonstration can clarify the task and reduce frustration. Physical guidance should be gentle and supportive, never corrective or forceful.

It is often helpful to break these exercises into smaller steps. Practicing one voice at a time, returning briefly to piano lid work, or reducing the number of repetitions can help the student regain confidence and clarity.

Teachers should resist the temptation to rush through threshold exercises. These moments form the foundation for future techniques. Time spent here often prevents much greater difficulty later.

When a threshold exercise begins to feel secure—when the movement feels stable, the sound remains calm, and the student shows less physical tension—it is a sign that the student is ready to move forward.

Threshold exercises are not obstacles to overcome quickly. They are **bridges** that support the students' transition to more complex technical and musical demands.

Preparing the Thumb

Preparation of the thumb is one of the most sensitive and essential aspects of early piano technique. In *Skillful Little Fingers*, thumb work is introduced gradually and without pressure, long before formal scales appear.

Rather than treating the thumb as a special or problematic finger, the method allows it to emerge **naturally as part of the hand's coordinated movement**. The thumb is never forced to pass under quickly or mechanically. Instead, it is invited to move when the hand is ready.

Early exercises help the student experience:

- a relaxed thumb position,
- freedom of movement without collapse,

- and smooth coordination with the longer fingers.

The idea of *Hide-and-Seek* is especially effective at this stage. The thumb briefly disappears under the hand and then returns, without urgency or strain. This playful image removes fear and helps the student accept the thumb's motion as something natural and gentle.

Teachers should observe the thumb. Signs of healthy thumb use include:

- a rounded, relaxed shape,
- movement supported by the hand and arm,
- and absence of gripping or pressing.

If the thumb collapses, stiffens, or becomes tense, it is appropriate to pause and return to earlier exercises that reinforce balance and freedom. Often, tension in the thumb reflects imbalance elsewhere in the hand.

Working away from the keyboard remains useful during this stage. Tapping motions and silent practice allow the student to explore the thumb-under movement without the added complexity of sound.

It is important to emphasize that thumb-under preparation does not mean mastering scales. At this point, the goal is familiarity and comfort, not speed or consistency. The student should feel that the thumb "belongs" in the movement.

By the time the first scale is introduced, the thumb-under motion should already feel familiar and unthreatening. The scale then becomes a continuation of an existing experience rather than a new technical challenge.

Why B Major Is the First Scale

The choice of B Major as the first scale in *Skillful Little Fingers* is deliberate and pedagogically grounded. Rather than beginning with a scale based on visual simplicity, this method prioritizes **physical comfort and natural hand alignment**.

In the B Major scale, most notes are played on the black keys. This supports the hand shape developed earlier through Chopin's Position, where the longer fingers rest naturally on the black keys and the thumb plays the white keys. As a result, the hand feels balanced and well-supported from the start.

Unlike scales that require frequent adjustments between white and black keys, the B Major scale allows the hand to maintain a consistent position. This reduces unnecessary movement and helps the student focus on **smooth motion, evenness, and connection,** rather than on searching for keys.

In this scale, the thumb plays only two white keys—B and E. These moments are clearly prepared through earlier thumb-under exercises and imagery such as *Hide-and-Seek*. When the scale is introduced, the thumb movement is already familiar and unthreatening.

For many students, B Major feels surprisingly comfortable. The keyboard itself guides the hand, providing tactile reference points that support accuracy and confidence. This experience helps reduce fear and resistance that are often associated with scale studies.

Introducing B Major first also reinforces an essential pedagogical message: scales are not obstacles to overcome but patterns of movement that grow naturally from coordinated technique.

By the time the student reaches the B Major scale, they have already experienced:

- balanced hand position,
- controlled finger independence,
- two voices within one hand,
- smooth legato motion,
- and gentle thumb-under preparation.

The scale is therefore not a new technical demand, but a familiar motion organized into a clear pattern. This approach establishes a positive and confident relationship with scale playing from the very beginning.

Signs of Readiness to Move Forward

Readiness to move forward in *Skillful Little Fingers* is not determined by tempo, speed, or the number of completed exercises. Instead, progress is measured by the **quality of movement, ease, and listening.**

A student may be considered ready to move on when the following signs are consistently present:

- the hand feels balanced and comfortable on the keyboard,
- the wrist moves freely without stiffness or collapse,
- the fingers respond easily rather than pressing or gripping,
- and the sound remains calm and controlled.

In threshold exercises, readiness often appears gradually. The student may begin to:

- hold long notes without visible tension,
- coordinate movement and sustained voices more smoothly,
- maintain legato while the hand shifts position,
- and approach thumb-under motion without hesitation.

It is important to note that occasional mistakes or unevenness do not indicate a lack of readiness. What matters is whether the student can recover balance easily and continue without strain.

Teachers should also observe the students' **listening**. Signs of readiness include the ability to notice:

- uneven sound,
- breaks in legato,
- or an imbalance between voices.

When a student begins to self-correct through listening rather than through instruction, meaningful progress is taking place.

Emotional readiness is equally important. A student who approaches exercises with curiosity rather than fear and is willing to try challenging material without resistance demonstrates readiness to move forward.

If progress feels unstable, it is appropriate to pause, revisit earlier material, or reduce the complexity of the task. Moving forward should feel like a natural continuation, not a forced step.

The goal of this book is not to advance quickly, but to advance **securely**. When the hand moves with ease, the sound remains free, and the student feels confident, the foundation for further technical and musical development is in place.

Common Difficulties and Gentle Corrections

As students work through *Skillful Little Fingers*, particular difficulties may appear from time to time. These challenges are a normal part of learning and do not indicate failure or poor ability. In most cases, they signal that the student is adjusting to new coordination or movement patterns.

The teacher's role is not to eliminate every difficulty immediately, but to respond **calmly, patiently, and with minimal intervention**.

Tension in the Hand or Wrist

If the hand or wrist appears stiff, it is often helpful to slow the tempo, reduce repetitions, or return briefly to an exercise on the piano lid. Gentle rocking or releasing motions can help restore flexibility. Avoid asking the student to "relax" without providing a physical solution.

Gripping or Pressing Fingers

When fingers press excessively into the keys, the underlying cause is often imbalance rather than weakness. Encouraging arm support, lighter touch, or shorter practice segments can help. Revisiting Chopin's Position usually restores balance quickly.

Collapsing Thumb

A collapsing thumb usually reflects tension elsewhere in the hand or arm. Instead of correcting the thumb directly, guide the student toward better overall balance. Returning to thumb-under preparation or Hide-and-Seek imagery can be especially effective.

Difficulty Holding Long Notes

If the student struggles to sustain long notes while other fingers move, simplify the task. Practice one voice at a time, reduce the tempo, or physically guide the hand. This difficulty often resolves naturally with repetition and patience.

Uneven Sound or Loss of *legato*

Unevenness is frequently associated with rushed movement or lack of attention. Encourage slower playing and attentive listening rather than relying on verbal instruction alone to correct. Counting aloud and using breath marks can help restore flow.

Resistance or Frustration

Emotional responses, such as hesitation or frustration, often emerge during threshold exercises. Acknowledge the difficulty and normalize it. Briefly returning to a familiar exercise can rebuild confidence before reattempting the challenge.

Over-Correction

One of the most common difficulties is excessive correction. Too many verbal instructions can overwhelm young students and increase tension. When possible, demonstrate the motion, gently guide the hand, or allow the student to explore and adjust through repetition.

Throughout the book, simplicity remains the guiding principle. When difficulties arise, the solution is usually found by returning to ease, clarity, and balance rather than adding complexity.

By responding to challenges with patience and gentle guidance, teachers help students develop trust in their own movement and sound. This approach fosters confidence, resilience, and a healthy relationship with piano technique that will support the student far beyond the first book.

Closing Note

Skillful Little Fingers, Book 1 is an invitation to slow down and listen—to the student's hand, to the quality of movement, and to the sound that emerges naturally from ease and balance.

This book does not seek quick results. Instead, it offers a foundation built on patience, clarity, and thoughtful guidance. When teachers allow students time to experience movement and gradually develop coordination, technique develops securely and without fear.

Every student's journey through this book will vary slightly. What matters most is not how quickly the pages are turned, but how comfortably the hand moves and how confidently the student listens.

Thank you for approaching this work with care and curiosity. Your presence, attention, and gentle guidance are essential parts of the learning process. Together, teacher and student build not only technical skills, but trust, awareness, and a lasting relationship with music.

A Note to Teachers and Parents

If this book has been helpful to you and your students, I would genuinely appreciate your feedback. Reviews help other teachers and families discover the book and understand how it is used in real lessons.

You are also very welcome to share your thoughts, questions, or teaching experiences with me directly.

reenayoung99@gmail.com

Thank you for the care and attention you bring to your students' musical journey.

— Reena Young

Glossary (Alphabetical Order)

Arm Drop
Using the natural weight of the arm to play a note without force or stiffness.

B Major
A scale with five black keys, often used to support natural hand position.

Bar Line
A vertical line that divides music into measures.

Breath Mark
A small comma in the music shows where the hand can gently lift, as if taking a breath.

Chopin's Position
A natural hand position in which the longer fingers rest on the black keys and the thumb and little finger stay on the white keys, creating balance, comfort, and freedom of movement.

Chord
Three or more notes played together.

Chromatic Scale
A scale built entirely of half steps, using all adjacent keys on the keyboard.

Cluster
A group of neighboring notes played together at the same time, creating a dense and colorful sound. Clusters are not "wrong notes" — they are a special sound.

Curved Fingers
A natural finger shape that helps produce a clear sound and prevents tension.

Double Bar Line
Two bar lines indicate a clear division or ending.

Finger Independence
The ability to move and control each finger separately.

Finger Numbers
Numbers are used to show which finger plays each note.
1 = thumb, 5 = little finger.

Flexible Wrist
A relaxed wrist that moves gently to help connect notes and support sound.

Forearm *Staccato*
A short, bouncing touch produced with help from the forearm, similar to bouncing a ball.

Four Notes per Stroke
Playing four notes connected by one flowing hand motion.

Home Position
The comfortable starting place of the hand on the keyboard before playing an exercise.

Legato
Playing notes smoothly and connected, without breaks between them.

***Legato–Staccato* Combination**
An articulation pattern where some notes are connected, and others are short.

Long *legato*
Maintaining a smooth connection over several notes or measures.

Measure
A group of beats in music, separated by bar lines.

Playing Two Notes Together
Playing two notes at the same time, like a small chord.

Quarter Rest
A symbol showing a silence that lasts for one beat.

Scale
A series of notes moving step by step up or down.

Slur
A curved line that shows which notes should be connected in a legato manner.

Staccato
Playing notes very short and detached, like touching something hot.

Stroke
A group of notes played with one coordinated movement of the hand or arm.

Three Notes per Stroke
Playing three notes smoothly with one coordinated movement.

Thumb Under
A scale technique in which the thumb passes under the hand to continue playing smoothly.

Thumb-Under Preparation

Exercises that gently prepare the thumb-under motion before learning scales.

Tie

A curved line that connects two notes of the same pitch, telling the player to hold the sound for the combined length of both notes.

Time Signature

A musical symbol that shows how many beats are in each measure.

Two Notes per Stroke

Playing two notes using one connected motion.

Two Voices in One Hand

Playing two musical lines within one hand, keeping each voice clear.

Two-Voice *legato*

Smooth, connected playing of two independent voices at the same time.

Voicing

Bringing out one voice while keeping another softer.

Wrist Roll

A small forward or side-to-side wrist motion used to connect notes smoothly.

Wrist Stroke

A controlled wrist movement used to produce sound, especially in light articulation.

CONGRATULATIONS!

Now you are ready for scales!

www.ingramcontent.com/pod-product-compliance
Lightning Source LLC
Chambersburg PA
CBHW041539120626
46551CB00019B/2757